THE
LETTER TO
THE
EPHESIANS

KEN FLEMING

Developed as a study course by Emmaus Correspondence School, founded in 1942.

The Letter to the Ephesians
Ken Fleming

Published by:

Emmaus Correspondence School
(A division of ECS Ministries)
PO Box 1028
Dubuque, IA 52004-1028
www.ecsministries.org

First Printing: 2007 (AK '07)

ISBN 978-1-59387-086-7

© 2007 ECS Ministries

Cover by Ragont Design, Barrington, IL

Printed in the United States of America

STUDENT INSTRUCTIONS

Lessons You Will Study

Course Components

This course has two parts: this study course and the exam booklet.

How to Study

This study has twelve chapters that will greatly help you. Each chapter has its own exam. Begin by asking God to open your heart to receive the truths He would teach you from His Word. Read the chapter through at least twice, once to get a general idea of its contents and then again, slowly, looking up all the Scripture references.

Begin studying immediately, or if you are in a group, as soon as the group begins. We suggest that you keep a regular schedule by trying to complete one chapter per week.

Exams

In the exam booklet there is one exam for each chapter (Exam 1 covers chapter 1 of the course). Do not answer the questions by what you think or have always believed. The questions are designed to find out if you understand the material and the Scripture verses given in the course.

After you have completed each chapter, review the related exam, and see how well you know the answers. If you find that you are having difficulty answering the questions, review the material until you think you can answer the questions.

How Your Exams are Graded

Your instructor will mark any incorrectly answered questions. You will be referred back to the place in the Bible or textbook where the correct answer is to be found. After finishing this course with a passing average, you will be awarded a certificate.

If you enrolled in a class, submit your exam papers to the leader or secretary of the class who will send them for the entire group to the Correspondence School.

See the back of the Exam Booklet for more information on returning the exams for grading.

INTRODUCTION

Paul's Letter to the Ephesians

The apostle Paul's letter to the Christians at Ephesus touches the pinnacle of biblical revelation concerning Christ in His role as the head of the church and the church in its role as the body of Christ. It reveals the great purpose and plan of God for the church as a worldwide community of believers in which His Spirit dwells. The letter begins with a section emphasizing theological truth and ends with a section that describes the duty of the readers in the light of that truth. The great church truths that are described in this letter may seem very lofty and beyond our ability to fully understand, but a grasp of them will help us live our day-to-day lives by giving us a clearer vision of what God is doing in this age.

The Author, Date, and Circumstances of Writing

Paul had made Ephesus the base of his evangelistic and teaching ministry for about three years, from AD 52 to AD 55. A strong church was planted in Ephesus, to be added to several others that had already been planted in the province of Asia. Five years had passed since he had been with them. At the time of writing, Paul was in prison, a fact he notes three times in the letter (3:1; 4:1; 6:20). The question is, during which of Paul's imprisonments did he write this letter? There are three possibilities. The first was his imprisonment in Caesarea, when Luke was with him. The second was in Rome, when Timothy and Epaphroditus were with him (Acts 24:27; 28:30). Most New Testament scholars believe that he was released from prison in Rome and spent a year or more visiting churches. They believe he was then rearrested in Troas and brought back to Rome, where he was again imprisoned until his execution by Nero.

It was almost certainly during his first Roman imprisonment that he wrote the four letters we call the "prison epistles": first Philippians, then Colossians, then Philemon, and finally Ephesians. The letter to the Ephesians was carried to them by Tychicus, who carried Paul's letters to the Colossians and Philemon at the same time (Ephesians 6:21-22; Colossians 4:7-8). The length of Paul's first imprisonment in Rome is calculated to be from the beginning of AD 60 to the end of AD 61.

The Recipients

Some scholars have questioned whether the church in Ephesus was actually the recipient because two of the earliest Greek manuscripts do not include the name Ephesus, and its content is more general in nature than Paul's other letters to churches. They suggest that the letter may have been a kind of circular letter intended for various churches in the province of Asia, including Ephesus. If Tychicus (the bearer of the letter) landed at the port city of Ephesus in the west and traveled overland to Colossae on the eastern edge of Asia it would have been necessary for him to pass by a number of cities where there were New Testament churches. It is not unreasonable to conclude that Paul intended that Tychicus read this letter to these local congregations, beginning with the church at Ephesus.

1

THE SCOPE OF OUR GREAT SALVATION

Ephesians 1:1-14

Paul the Apostle (v. 1)

Paul establishes his credentials in the first verse as "an apostle of Jesus Christ by the will of God." The title, as used here, indicates a person called and sent by Christ as a fully authorized messenger to preach and teach truths related to the gospel and church truth while the church was being founded. Note the order of Christ's names in this verse: "Christ Jesus." Paul never knew Christ in the flesh and consistently used His title *Christ* before his personal name *Jesus,* unlike Peter, James, and John, who mostly referred to Him as "Jesus Christ." Paul's apostleship was by the "will of God": God had revealed to Paul from the day of his conversion that He had chosen him to take the name of the Lord Jesus to Gentiles, kings, and the nation of Israel (Acts 9:15).

Paul's Readers

Paul refers to his readers in Ephesus first as "saints" (v. 1). The word *saint* means "one who is set apart," or "a holy one." It is a common term for believers in the New Testament, because all believers are set apart for God. It does not indicate a special status attained by a few outstanding Christians who do some remarkable work. As saints we should live for Him rather than for unholy, worldly goals. We do not become saints by being saintly, but we should be saintly because we are saints.

The second way Paul describes his readers is as the "faithful in Christ Jesus." This does not mean they were a special class of Christians who were more faithful than others; rather, it describes all those who have put their faith in Christ Jesus as their Savior. We should pay particular attention to the phrase, "in Christ Jesus." It is a key phrase in the epistle to the Ephesians and refers to Christ as *the spiritual sphere in which believers live*. When God the Father sees us in Christ, He no longer sees us as guilty sinners but as righteous because we are now identified with His beloved Son. We are, therefore, fit for His presence.

The Greeting (v. 2)

Paul's greeting combines the idea of *grace* from the Greek greeting of the first century and *peace* from the Hebrew greeting used since the time of Abraham. When he invokes *grace* for his readers, Paul is not speaking of "saving" grace but of "enabling" grace—God's divine help. He wants them to experience God's help and strength in their daily lives—for deliverance from evil, for victory over sin, and for strength to serve others. It is the grace that Christ dispenses at the "throne of grace" in response to our asking (Hebrews 4:16). In addition to grace, Paul desires *peace* for them. He is not speaking of peace *with* God, when the enmity between us and God was removed by the finished work of Christ at the cross. He is speaking of the peace *of* God, which is the sense of calmness and confidence that the believer can enjoy in all the circumstances of life. It is the peace *of* God that guards and protects our hearts (Philippians 4:7).

The source of grace and peace is "God our Father and the Lord Jesus Christ." The title "our Father" emphasizes His nearness and relationship to us as believers. He becomes our Father when we are born again, born spiritually (John 1:12-13; 3:3). The title "Lord Jesus Christ" is God the Son's full title: as *Lord* He is the sovereign Lord and Master; as *Jesus* He is the Man who lived, died, and rose again; as the *Christ* He is the anointed Messiah, the one chosen and sent by God to fulfill God's mission. Notice in these first two verses that the apostle, the saints, and the greeting are all centered in Christ: Paul is the apostle *of* Christ; the Ephesians are saints *in* Christ; both grace and peace come to believers *from* Christ.

God's Eternal Plan (vv. 3-14)

Paul's heart overflows as he thinks about the scope of God's eternal plan of salvation. He begins by expressing praise and worship to God for the blessings that derive from His gracious heart. Paul wrote verses as one long sentence in which he explains some aspe plan of salvation. These include expressions of worship concerni and the activities of God the Father, God the Son, and God the Holy Spirit, which tumble over one another in cascades of praise. Three times Paul comes to a climax in his review of the blessings of God's grace with the words, "to the praise of His glory" (vv. 6, 12, 14).

He begins with a kind of doxology in which he *blesses* God for having *blessed* His people with every spiritual *blessing* (v. 3). When God blesses us, He bestows His goodness on us. When we bless Him, we praise Him for His goodness and for the magnitude of the blessings He has granted us. We bless God as "the God and Father of our Lord Jesus Christ." This name is appropriate, for it is only through His Son that believers have access to the Father, who is the source of the blessings we receive.

The Sphere of Our Spiritual Blessings (v. 3)

The blessings the Father has freely showered on all His people are spiritual benefits. They are spiritual in the sense that they are non-material. We may appropriate and enjoy them as we progress in our walk with God. *How* we appropriate them may be illustrated by the way that the children of Israel obtained their God-given blessings in the days of Joshua. God blessed them by granting them the land of Canaan, but they did not enjoy the blessings of the land until they appropriated it. This they did by moving into the land, trusting in God to give them victory by driving out their enemies, step by step. In this way they claimed it through faith and progressively occupied it by obeying God (Joshua 1:2-3; see also Deuteronomy 28:1-12).

Our spiritual blessings include the enjoyment of the truths related to our wonderful salvation described in the following verses. These truths pertain to the work of the Spirit of God in us. When we claim these truths by faith and resist any influence that would keep us from enjoying them, they become the source of uncounted blessings, independent of our circumstances on earth.

What are the "heavenly places"?

Note carefully that the spiritual blessings are not on earth, but "in heavenly places," sometimes termed "the heavenlies." (Notice that, in the New King James Version, the word "places" is in italics, indicating that this word is not

THE LETTER TO THE EPHESIANS

in the Greek manuscript.) The term only appears in Ephesians. From the five times it is used we learn that the heavenly places are:

- ✓ where our spiritual blessings exist and are enjoyed (1:3).

- ✓ where Christ has been granted power to rule (1:20).

- ✓ where believers as one entity are secure with Christ (2:6).

- ✓ where angelic principalities and powers exist (3:10).

- ✓ where our conflict takes place against spiritual hosts of wickedness (6:12).

In summary we may say that the heavenly places are the sphere where believers are united with Christ and where they experience both spiritual blessings and spiritual battles. The heavenly places are not heaven itself, although they are the realm where heaven rules. We as believers in Christ are able to experience life in the heavenlies while we live here on earth. Because we are in Christ in the heavenly places we are to deliberately focus on the spiritual aspects of our life there. Paul wrote to the Colossians, "Set your mind on things above, not on things on the earth. For . . . your life is hidden with Christ in God" (Colossians 3:2-3).

Chosen in Christ (v. 4)

The first of our spiritual blessings in this remarkable list is the fact that God the Father "chose us *in Him* [Christ] before the foundation of the world," that is, before creation (v. 4, emphasis added; Colossians 1:16). This truth about His choosing us in Christ is called the doctrine of election. God's sovereign choice of us was designed for Christ and accomplished through Him. Just as Israel is God's *chosen nation* (Isaiah 45:4) and Jesus the Messiah was His *chosen Servant* (Isaiah 42:1) to accomplish the work of salvation, so the church is His *chosen people*. In 1 Peter 2:9 we are called a "chosen generation." God determined to bring us to Himself through His Son. God's motivation for choosing (or electing) us lies within His gracious and loving nature.

Although we cannot fully understand it, we should respond to this spiritual blessing with humble worship. We should resist the temptation to conclude that God also chose others to eternal punishment. Not one word in Scripture supports this unbiblical idea. We should simply rejoice in what the all-wise God has revealed. Election has nothing to do with our worth, nor is God in any way arbitrary or capricious. It is a wonderful spiritual blessing that God chose us in His Son.

Chosen for a Purpose

The purpose for which God chose His people in Christ is that we should be "holy and without blame before Him," that we should be completely sanctified (v. 4). Paul had already addressed the Ephesians as "saints," or holy ones. Now he tells them that God long ago *chose* them to be holy. Christ presents them, as saved ones, to the Father as "holy and blameless in His sight" because He has reconciled them to God through His own blood (Colossians 1:20-22). In heaven, holiness will be fully realized as the goal of election. In the meantime, believers today are to progressively become more like Christ, to be "blameless in holiness" while they await His coming (1 Thessalonians 3:13). One of the great evidences of our election is that we are striving for holiness and blamelessness (Romans 12:1).

The words "in love" at the end of verse 4 can be understood in two ways; they either modify "holy and without blame" in verse 4 or "having predestined us" in verse 5. Commentators are divided. If they are connected with our adoption as sons in verse 5 it would mean that in love God predestined us to adoption as sons. It seems more likely that the words "in love" modify "holy and without blame," meaning that our love is to be without blame. One reason for preferring this view is that the other five uses of "in love" in Ephesians all refer to human love, not God's love (cf. 3:17; 4:2, 15, 16; 5:2). It makes perfectly good sense that believers should evidence their holiness and blamelessness before God in the realm of their love for Him and His people.

Predestined to Adoption as Sons (v. 5)

Another one of our spiritual blessings is that God predestined us to adoption as sons. Predestination is more than simple choice; it is the choice to a destiny (pre-destined). God has destined us to be adopted as sons (not children) into the family of God, with all the status, privilege, and responsibilities of mature, adult sonship (Galatians 4:4-7). We become *children of God* by being regenerated (born again) by God's Spirit. We become *sons of God* by being adopted and placed in a position to receive the benefits of adult sonship.

In the Roman culture, adoption of a slave into a wealthy family implied granting him all the privileges of sonship, especially related to inheritance. As believers, we do not have to wait until Christ reigns in glory to enjoy our spiritual inheritance. In Christ we can enjoy *now* the multitude of blessings that the Father has bestowed upon us. We can bask in the sunshine of truths such as election, justification, forgiveness, redemption, and reconciliation. By doing this we grow in appreciation of our relationship to God.

With honored status in God's family, believers can confidently approach the infinite God as their Father, not just as Lord and Master. This truth alone ought to stimulate all believers to praise and worship. It is incredible that the God of creation wanted to share this father-son relationship with us! God's action in predetermining us to be His sons was done "according to the good pleasure of His will" (v. 5). His "will" speaks of what He purposed or intended. His "good pleasure" refers to the delight He took in giving us the status of sonship. As His sons we are being conformed to the image of His beloved Son (2 Corinthians 3:18). When we get to heaven, our conformity to His image will be complete (Romans 8:29).

As Paul considers the blessings of God's choice of us in eternity past and our predestination to be His sons, he exclaims, "to the praise of the glory of His grace" (v. 6). It is an expression of awe at the enormity of God's amazing grace in redeeming people who were slaves to sin and then adopting them to be His full sons. *Grace* refers to God's unmerited favor toward us, and nowhere does it shine more brightly than in the truth that before the world began He chose us who were unworthy sinners to be in Christ, and that He destined us to be full sons. God "accepted" us "in the Beloved," that is, in Christ, the supreme object of His love. Because God the Father fully accepts His pure and perfect Son, He fully accepts us too, because we are now in Christ.

"Redemption through His blood" (v. 7)

In addition to being "accepted in the Beloved," Paul enumerates several more blessings that belong to believers. The first of these is *redemption*, which means "deliverance by the payment of a price." Redemption is an Old Testament truth from the experience of the Israelites. They were slaves of Pharaoh in Egypt until God "redeemed" them with His mighty hand (Deuteronomy 7:8). God delivered them from bondage. In the New Testament both the Lord Jesus and the apostle Paul viewed believers as redeemed from the bondage of our cruel master called sin (John 8:34-36; Romans 3:24). Christ our Redeemer accomplished our redemption by the payment of a price, a ransom which was nothing less than His own blood (1 Peter 1:18-19). He paid the price so that we could be released from sin's bondage.

Closely linked with our redemption is *forgiveness*. The Lord Jesus linked redemption and forgiveness when He instituted the Lord's Supper. He took the cup and gave thanks saying, "This is my blood of the new covenant, which is shed for many for the remission [forgiveness] of sins" (Matthew 26:28). Redemption and forgiveness are closely related because both carry the idea of release of the sinner from an impossible predicament. Redemption releases us by the payment of a price for our sin; forgiveness releases us by the granting of a pardon for our sin. Forgiveness of our sins is made possible because the redemption price has been paid. Both are accomplished "by the riches of His grace."

Paul continues to exalt the riches of God's grace to us by explaining how He "made it abound"—that is, He lavished it on us extravagantly (v. 8). In bestowing the wealth of His grace on us, God does so "in all wisdom and prudence" or understanding. He gives believers these gifts so that they may discern and enjoy something of His purpose for them and the position that they have been granted in Christ. In writing to the Colossians, Paul prays that they may be filled with "wisdom and spiritual understanding" (Colossians 1:9). May God give us growing insight into the limitless wealth of His grace that He lavishes on us.

"The mystery of His will" (vv. 9-10)

A further blessing God has given believers is to know that both their calling in the *past* and their redemption in the *present* are part of His purpose for the whole universe in the *future*. This purpose is called "the mystery of His will."

A *mystery* in the New Testament is "a truth previously unknown but now revealed." The mystery revealed here is that God's plans for the future include—and in fact are centered on—Christ and the church. God's "will" regarding this mystery is progressing toward a planned climax. The completion of God's purpose for believers is called the "dispensation of the fullness of times." (The word "dispensation" refers to a stage in history administered [that is, dispensed] by God.) The present dispensation is called the dispensation of grace. The "fullness of the times" is the period following the present dispensation of God's dealing with mankind in grace [3:2].

In the fullness of time, God will "gather together in one all things in Christ" (v. 10). The Greek word for gather is only used one other time in the New Testament, where the Ten Commandments are all "summed up" in the saying, "You shall love your neighbor as yourself" (Romans 13:9). Our verse tells us that everything in heaven and earth will be summed up in Christ. At present there are discordant elements as a result of sin. But in the fullness of the times, everything in the universe will be brought into harmony with Christ as the head when all things are united "in Him." Christ is already the head of the church, but in a coming day the purpose of God will come to fruition with Him as the head of the whole universe. When we, as believers in Christ, grasp something of the astounding and magnificent glory that will surround our Savior, every thought, word, and action of our lives should become worship.

Believers are God's Heritage (vv. 11-12)

Verse 11 begins, "in whom also we have obtained an inheritance." All agree that "in whom" refers to Christ. Commentators do not agree, however, whether the next phrase should be translated as in our text or whether it should read, "in whom we were made a heritage" as in the NIV and others. Both translations are possible and both statements are true. But it seems better to see it here as the second option because the focus in the passage is on *God's purchased possession* (v. 14) and *His inheritance in the saints* (v. 18). The idea of believers being the "heritage of God" flows out of the Old Testament context where Israel, and only Israel, is often seen as God's heritage (Deuteronomy 32:9; Psalm 33:12; etc.). In the New Testament, particularly in this book, we learn that God's heritage is made up of both believing Jews and believing Gentiles.

Paul goes on to say that the heritage of God, made up of redeemed Jews and Gentiles, was foreordained "according to the purpose of Him who works all things according to the counsel of His will" (v. 11). His purpose from the beginning was that this should be so, and whatever He purposed is certain to be fulfilled. Nothing can frustrate God's will. He works out everything by His wisdom and power so that it conforms to His purpose. The classic illustration of this is seen in salvation, which was accomplished through the betrayal, trial, and crucifixion of Christ. Out of suffering and death came all the blessings of our salvation. Believers can be certain, therefore, that when Christ is the head of the universe, His purpose to make them His heritage will be fulfilled.

When believers become the heritage of God, His glory shining in them will be admired by the entire universe to "the praise of His glory" (see 2:7). Paul speaks first of the Jewish believers like himself, the "we" who first trusted, or put their hope in, Christ (v. 12). Then he speaks of Gentile believers, the "you" who also "trusted [in Christ], after you heard the word of truth, the gospel of your salvation" (v. 13). God's order was to offer salvation to the Jew first, then the Greek (or Gentile; see Romans 1:16). Following Christ's resurrection, almost all of the earliest believers were Jews. It was several years before evangelistic attention was paid to the Gentiles (Acts 11:19; 13:46). The mention of both Jewish and Gentile believers introduces one of the main themes of Ephesians: that both groups are united into one body as equals.

"Sealed with the Holy Spirit of promise" (v. 13)

The next spiritual blessing enumerated by Paul is being *sealed* with the Holy Spirit of promise (v. 13). In this context the sealing marks those "having believed" as belonging to God. Property deeds were often sealed with a wax-like substance into which the owner's signet was pressed before it hardened. The impression in the wax identified it as belonging to him (Jeremiah 32:44). God has given to all believers the Holy Spirit as a seal to identify them as belonging to Him (2 Corinthians 1:22; Romans 8:9). With this seal we are secure in Christ. The Holy Spirit is called the "Spirit of promise" because the Lord Jesus promised the disciples that after His departure He would send the Holy Spirit as a Helper to "abide with them forever" (John 14:16; 15:26).

"The guarantee of our inheritance" (v. 14)

In addition to the fact that the Holy Spirit is a *seal*, He is also the *guarantee* or, better, the *down payment* of our coming inheritance. When we are aware of the comfort, encouragement, help, peace, and joy that He provides to us as believers, we can be assured that this experience is just the beginning. The Spirit of God provides a down payment of what it will be like in the glorified life that is our inheritance to come, just as an engagement ring is to the bride both a down payment and a guarantee of her coming marriage. Thus the present ministry of the Holy Spirit that brings us comfort and guidance in this life is both a foretaste and a guarantee of coming glory. We enjoy the "first fruits of the Spirit" now, but the full harvest is still to come (Romans 8:23).

What is in store for us is called "the redemption of the purchased possession." In the context of this passage, it is applied to both Jews and Gentiles. We can understand the idea better when we remember that in Old Testament times Israel was called God's "special treasure" or possession (Exodus 19:5; Malachi 3:17). Here we learn the remarkable truth that both Jewish and Gentile believers are already God's purchased possession, although the full reality of it is still future (cf. Acts 20:28; 1 Peter 2:9). At that future time, the praise of His glory will be complete.

Looking back over the first fourteen verses of Ephesians we have learned that the *cause* of our salvation was the good pleasure of God's will before the foundation of the world. As a result we have been redeemed, forgiven, and accepted in Christ. We have also learned that the *reason* God has saved us was for His own honor: for "the praise of the glory of His grace." God's purpose began in eternity past *to the praise of His glory* (v. 6); it will culminate when everything is summed up in Christ *to the praise of His glory* (vv. 9-12); our salvation is guaranteed by the Holy Spirit *to the praise of His glory* (v. 14).

We will be blessed by meditating on these truths and growing in appreciation for what God has done for us in and through Christ.

2

PAUL'S PRAYER FOR WISDOM AND REVELATION

Ephesians 1:15-23

Paul had a big heart for all believers—not just his own immediate circle—and he was concerned that they grow in their spiritual understanding. Some of them had come to Christ directly from his ministry when he spent three years in Ephesus. Others came to Christ through believers in the surrounding cities of Asia where there were newly planted churches. He did not know them all personally, but he was thrilled nonetheless with the work of God's transforming grace. In the light of all the spiritual blessings that he has just listed in the first portion of chapter 1 he now turns his attention to praying for all these believers.

Their Faith and Love (vv. 15-16)

Paul had heard two things about them that verified the reality of their salvation: their continuing faith and their genuine love for all the saints (v. 15). Paul thanked God for them every time he mentioned them in his prayers. He prayed for individuals who had been saved and the assemblies that had been formed. What a prayer list he must have had! In his continual prayers and thanksgiving for other believers he is an outstanding example to us. We get a glimpse of one key prayer in the next few verses.

Prayer to the Father of Glory (v. 17)

Paul's prayer moves from *praise* to *petition*. He addresses his prayer to "the God of our Lord Jesus Christ, the Father of glory." Paul calls Him "the Father of glory" because he wants to emphasize the unique glory of

od's Fatherhood. Just as the King of glory is the "one unique King," even
.10ugh there are many other kings, so the Father of glory is the "one unique
Father." It is to Him that all glory belongs.

A Prayer for Knowledge (v. 17)

Paul prays first that God will give to them the "spirit of wisdom and
revelation in the knowledge of Him" (v. 17). He asks the Father to grant
these requests to them that they may know God better. It is impossible to
know God unless He reveals Himself. There is debate among commentators
as to whether the word "spirit" refers to the Holy Spirit of God or to a
spiritual attitude, such as the "spirit of faith" or the "spirit of meekness" (2
Corinthians 4:13; Galatians 6:1). It seems better to understand that he is
speaking of the Holy Spirit, because "no one knows the things of God except
the Spirit of God" (1 Corinthians 2:11). Thus He is called the "Spirit of
wisdom and revelation." He is "the Spirit of wisdom" because He provides
wisdom to believers (Isaiah 11:2). Wisdom is the proper use of knowledge;
it gives us the ability to understand how to think and act in a situation so as
to please God. The Holy Spirit is also the "Spirit of revelation" in that He
reveals the "deep things of God" (1 Corinthians 2:9-10).

Paul recorded four outstanding prayers in the Prison Epistles to churches.
In all of them, a key theme is that growth in knowledge is essential to
spiritual growth. He prays that they may "know" (v. 18), "comprehend"
(3:18), and have "knowledge" (Philippians 1:9; Colossians 1:9). When
believers study the Scriptures, the indwelling Holy Spirit gives spiritual
discernment to help them grasp the implications of the truths they are reading.
The Greek word for knowledge in verse 17 is a strong one, implying intimate
knowledge. To know something of the nature of God is to know something
of the most exalted of all subjects. It is the Holy Spirit who gives clearer and
deeper insight concerning the truth about God from His Word.

Knowing God is more than simply knowing about Him by our study and
conclusions. He reveals Himself to us primarily through His Word but also
through prayer, worship, and fellowship with Him. Just as we come to know
people by spending time with them in a variety of situations, we come to
know God in the same way. The more we know Him, the more eager we
are to please Him. In His Great High Priestly Prayer, the Lord Jesus Christ
prayed that we might know God (John 17:3). There is probably no greater
need for the church today than the need to know God the Father and God
the Son by means of the Holy Spirit.

A Prayer for Spiritual Vision (vv. 18-19)

The condition into which this growing knowledge of God brings believers is *spiritual insight*: "the eyes of your understanding being enlightened." The word "understanding" in the Greek text is the word for *heart*, by which the Greeks meant the center of their personality, including their intelligence and will. Paul refers to the heart as if it had eyes and could see spiritual things. He prays that the floodlight of the Holy Spirit might shine on those things so that believers could see them better and appreciate them. All believers receive the Holy Spirit at the time of their conversion. It is the work of the Spirit to give them a deeper understanding of the things of God.

When the hearts of these Ephesians (and all believers) are enlightened by the Spirit of God they understand three important truths concerning God and His people. Each of them begins with the word "what" in our text (vv. 18-19). Many Christians fail to see these spiritual realities because they are so earthbound. Few Christians ever pray that they might have their eyes opened to see them. They are like the servant of the prophet Elisha who could not see the protecting hosts of God surrounding them until Elisha prayed, "O Lord I pray, open his eyes that he may see" (2 Kings 6:17). In this same way, Paul prays that we might know these spiritual realities and be strengthened in our spirits as a result. The realities concern God's calling, God's inheritance, and God's power—spiritual realities that are not experienced intellectually or emotionally.

"The hope of His calling" (v. 18)

The first request is that believers might have a better vision of the "hope of His calling," or the hope for which God has called us. His calling began with His choice of us before the foundation of the world (v. 4). At that point we were also predestined to adoption as sons (v. 5). Our calling became effective when we responded by faith in Christ. The hope of our calling looks forward to our eventual destiny in Christ. That destiny is our sure hope of appearing with Christ in glory when He returns for us.

This hope is far more than a longing for the eventual triumph of good over evil. It is the "hope of the glory of God" (Romans 5:2). At that time not only will we appear with Christ in glory; Christ will also be glorified in His saints (Colossians 3:4, 2 Thessalonians 1:10). The prayer is that we will gain an increased understanding of this hope so that we will live with eternity's values in view. When we do that, we will be encouraged in a discouraging world with the certain hope that God's program of the ages will climax in God's glory.

"The glory of His inheritance in the saints" (v. 18)

The second request is that God would open the eyes of our hearts to see "the riches of the glory of His inheritance in the saints." Although it is possible to understand this second request as looking forward to what *we* receive when we are glorified, it is better to see it as referring to the glory *God* receives when we are glorified. "*His* inheritance" refers to those whom He called to Himself. So Paul prayed that we might appreciate the glory God will receive when the completed church becomes His inheritance.

Can there be any higher incentive to live in the light of the glory of God? Believers are already God's "purchased possession" as indicated in verse 14. Thus He places infinite value on those that Christ redeemed for God. Paul wants us to see how highly God values His "possession"—the church, His special treasure, worth more to Him than uncounted worlds in space. Believers that comprise the church are His trophies of grace and reflect His own glory. It is a staggering thought that when Christ comes again He will be glorified in His saints.

"The exceeding greatness of His power" (v. 19)

Paul has prayed that we might understand the *wonderful hope* that we have because God has called us, and that we might understand the *incomparable glory* that God will inherit when the church is complete. Paul now prays that we will understand the *immense power* at work for us who believe. To describe this power he uses four different Greek words. These could be paraphrased as power, energy, strength, and might. In addition to these descriptions he speaks of the *greatness* of that power, and to that he adds the *exceeding* greatness of it. Paul goes to the outer limits of language to describe it.

Note that the power is not available to unbelievers, but for us who believe. We were saved when we believed that God "raised Christ from the dead" (Romans 10:9). As we grow in our Christian experience, we come to appreciate His power in our lives. We can experience His power when we overcome temptation to sin in thought, word, or deed. His power is also seen when we find strength to face difficulties, when we find grace to bear with others who sin against us, and when we find courage to uphold the name of Christ and His gospel in a hostile world. It enables us to be "more than conquerors through Him who loved us" (Romans 8:37). It is this kind of power that Paul prays we might experience.

The Power of His Resurrection (v. 20)

Paul does not detail what the power does until his second prayer in chapter 3. This much is clear here: we should never be satisfied with mere orthodoxy, where there is no power to transform people's lives. Paul then draws our attention to the most dramatic display of God's power, which He demonstrated when He raised Christ out from among the dead. Just as the death of Christ is the superlative expression of the love of God, so the resurrection of Christ is the superlative expression of the power of God. It was the greatest demonstration of power in the history of the universe, even greater than the power of creation. It defeated the combined hosts of hell who were trying to keep Christ in the tomb. Christ's resurrection was a public demonstration of Satan's defeat.

The Glory of Christ's Ascension (v. 20)

In the preaching of the early church, the resurrection and the ascension were placed side by side in importance (cf. Acts 2:32-33). At Pentecost, Peter declared that the resurrection was fulfilled prophecy by quoting Psalm 16:10 (Acts 2:27). He went on to say that the ascension was also fulfilled prophecy by quoting Psalm 110:1 (Acts 2:34). Not only was God's power demonstrated in Christ's resurrection, it was further demonstrated in His ascension and exaltation to His own right hand in heaven. The "right hand of God" indicates the place of *privilege* (Hebrews 1:13), *power* (Matthew 26:64), and *dominion* (1 Peter 3:22). Here we see that the heavenly places is the spiritual sphere where Christ is enthroned with supreme honor and authority.

The Superiority of His Rule (vv. 21-22)

Enthroned in the heavenly places, Christ is "far above all principality and power and might and dominion and every name that is named." These designations of authority refer to various orders of angelic beings, including Satan's demonic hosts. The same categories are referred to as the "spiritual hosts of wickedness in the heavenly places" (6:12). These and other passages using similar language make it unlikely that mere human government is in view here (cf. 3:10; Colossians 1:16; 1 Peter 3:22).

Other passages such as Revelation 1:5 make it clear that Christ has been appointed by God to be "the ruler over the kings of the earth." The ascended Christ is exalted above all others, no matter what names they take or whether they live in this age or in that which is to come. The age to come was inaugurated by His resurrection and will be consummated in the future. By that time He will have made a reality of having all things "under his feet." It was the practice in ancient times for kings to place their feet on the necks of enemies they captured to symbolize their complete victory over them. Other references to Christ exercising His sovereign power in the future by putting His enemies under His feet are Psalm 8:6, 1 Corinthians 15:23-28, Hebrews 2:8, and Hebrews 10:13.

Christ is the Head of the Church (vv. 22-23)

In addition to placing the Lord Jesus Christ above all principality and power in His ascended glory, God the Father also declares Christ's power over all things for the church (v. 22). He had been appointed to be the supreme head of the church. The church is composed of all true believers in this age from the day of Pentecost until the time when they are taken up to be with Him at the rapture (1 Thessalonians 4:13-18). As the head of the church He claims all authority and rule over the church. It is wrong for any human leader to claim this authority.

In verse 23, the idea of Christ as head of the church is taken one step further. Not only is Christ the head in the sense of *being its ruler*, He is also its head in the sense of *being in relationship to it as His body*. He functions as its living head. He plans, coordinates, unifies, directs, and controls, just as our physical heads function in relation to our bodies. Thus Jesus Christ is the living head of His living body. Paul uses this imagery a number of times in the New Testament (Romans 12:5; 1 Corinthians 12:12). As the head and body are part of one entity, so are Christ and the church.

Finally, the church is described as "the fullness" of Christ and Christ is described as "Him who fills all in all" or the one who fills the universe (v. 22). To think of these two ideas together is, perhaps, more than we can fully grasp with our minds, but the metaphor of the head and body helps us. The body is the necessary complement to the head. The body of the exalted Christ is the vehicle through which He carries out His will.

The implications of these truths for us are enormous and can revolutionize our Christian lives and our churches. When our eyes are opened to know God the Father of the Lord Jesus Christ we will better understand His purpose that He fulfilled in Christ and what our part is. We will see the grandeur of our hope, the glory of His inheritance in us, and the greatness of His power. Thus we shall serve Him with greater enthusiasm. We will present ourselves to Him as Lord when we realize that He is far above every power on earth or in heaven. We will confidently face the opposition confronting us because He is the ascended Victor who has been given authority over all beings in heaven and on earth and who is destined to reign over the universe. Finally, we will worship with enlightened hearts when we understand that we believers have been incorporated into the body of Him who fills all in all.

3

SALVATION BY GRACE THROUGH FAITH

Ephesians 2:1-10

The subject in chapter 2 flows right out of the truth about Christ's resurrection (1:20). Paul now enlarges on this truth to say that not only did God raise Christ from the dead by His mighty power, but He also raised them, as believers, from their old condition of spiritual death to their new elevated condition of spiritual life in the risen Christ.

This chapter describes the *vertical* ascent of salvation experience, from the valley of death to the peak of glory. It compares to the *horizontal* progress of salvation history that began in eternity past and progresses to eternity future. In all of human experience, there is no greater distance than the distance between death and life. Paul takes us on an upward journey from the depths of our spiritual death to the heights of our spiritual life in Christ.

"And you He made alive" (v. 1)

He begins by reminding the Ephesians that they had been made alive in Christ. Note that the words "He made alive" are in italics in our Bible text, which indicates that they do not appear in the Greek manuscript. They are borrowed from verse 5 and inserted in verse 1 to make the English translation read more smoothly. Between these two verses Paul launches into an extended explanation of how we acted as "dead people" before we were saved. We should clearly understand that God has made us alive from being spiritually dead. He has "delivered us from the power of darkness and translated us into the kingdom of the Son of His love" (Colossians 1:13).

"Dead in trespasses and sins" (v. 1)

In sharp contrast to their *present condition* with the glorified Christ in the heavenly places, Paul now diagnoses their *former condition* before they were saved. At that time they were "dead in trespasses and sins." Far worse than being sick with sin and needing personal reform or special treatment, they were absolutely dead spiritually. A spiritually dead person has no sensitivities to the things of God—spiritual things. They mean nothing to him and he cannot respond to them. This is the unfortunate state of every unsaved person.

Every person without Christ is dead, and there are no exceptions (Romans 3:23; 6:23). Paul goes on to describe the environment in which these Ephesian believers were once dead spiritually. It was an environment of rebellion against God. "Trespasses" are violations against God's order, while the term "sins" is more general and refers to anything that falls short of God's perfect standard. Paul was saying that in the realm of spiritual death, trespasses and sins are the governing principle. A person may be intelligent, capable, witty, likeable, skilled, and highly regarded and yet have no interest in God or spiritual things. He may do service in his community and attend church, but he is missing the mark of God's glory. That kind of person may be much more desirable than a criminal as a neighbor in the community, but without Christ he is spiritually just as dead as any other wicked or ungodly non-believer.

"Walked according to the course of this world" (v. 2)

Paul reminds the Gentile believers in Ephesus that before they were saved they were in a state of spiritual death: they "walked according to the course of this world." In this way they acted as the living dead. Whether consciously or unconsciously, they had been shaped by the value system of the "present evil age" (Galatians 1:4). The word "world," as used in the New Testament, refers to the order or system of things in culture and society from which God is left out (except when it refers to the world of people, as in John 3:16, for example). People are influenced by the world system through media, education, politics, society, entertainment, and other avenues of culture. Those without Christ are its captives.

Satan, the Prince of the Power of the Air

The believers in Ephesus had not only once walked according to the course of this world but "according to the prince of the power of the air" (v. 2). This "prince," whose title is sometimes translated "the ruler of the kingdom of the air," dominates the world system. He is Satan, also known as "the ruler of this world" (John 12:31) and "the god of this age" (2 Corinthians 4:4). He rules over an enormous, unseen army of angelic beings called demons (Matthew 9:34). The "air" is a figure of speech that indicates the sphere in which Satan's demons carry on their evil duties. Through them Satan influences people in their lives, homes, governments, and institutions of every kind to try to thwart the great purpose of God, which is to redeem people and glorify His Son.

"Sons of disobedience" (v. 2)

Our text speaks of "the spirit *who* now works in the sons of disobedience," meaning that Satan is that spirit (v. 2, emphasis added). Other versions have "the spirit *that* is now working," referring to what characterizes the followers of Satan, which is disobedience to God. For this reason they are called "sons of disobedience," Satan being their spiritual father (John 8:44). In their unbelief they have no regard for God's Word or God's ways. Note also that the spirit of disobedience is *now* working; that same spirit is as active today as it was in Paul's day. This anti-God spirit pervades the entire world system. It is seen in many ways, including the persecution of believers, corruption in business and government, moral perversion, animosity between neighbors, and divisions in churches.

"The lusts of our flesh" (v. 3)

Having reminded the Ephesians that when they were spiritually dead they were dominated by two powerful influences (the evil world system and Satan with his army of demons), Paul now turns to the third dominating influence in their "walk" as dead people: the flesh. Notice that Paul here uses the word "we," including himself as being one of the "sons of disobedience" who conducted himself in the lusts of the flesh. "Lusts" are simply "desires." "The flesh" refers to the sinful or fallen nature in all people. The lusts of the flesh are the desires of the sinful nature. When we gratify them, it is in opposition to God. Some of these are in our minds and remain there, such as pride or, to use an extreme example, addiction to pornography. Others are acted out in our bodies, such as bullying or sexual sin. Because they work in both mind and body, Paul calls them the "desires of the flesh and of the mind."

Paul concludes that those who are spiritually dead are "by nature children of wrath" (v. 3). Not only have they *committed* many sins under the influence of the world, the devil, and the flesh, but they are sinners by nature. Every person on earth since Adam and Eve, with the exception of Jesus, was born in sin. And being born in sin we are by nature the children of wrath. This means that we are the objects of God's righteous anger and His eternal judgment. God is justly angry at sin and must, therefore, judge all sinners. Until we believe in God's Son, "the wrath of God abides on them [us]" (John 3:36). Note that verse 3 includes Jews and Gentiles. It begins by referring to "we all," that is, people like Paul, who was a religious Jew. It goes on to point out that they were the children of wrath just as the "others"— the Gentiles. Paul declares categorically, "There is none righteous, no, not one" (Romans 3:10). The conclusion is that all people are under the wrath of God by their actions and by their nature.

"But God" (v. 4)

After the terrible news in the first three verses, that all people are born spiritually dead and are the deserving objects of God's eternal judgment, comes the best and most wonderful news. We call it *the gospel*, the good news. It is introduced with two simple words that change the message of God's wrath to a message of God's favor: "But God." These words convert condemnation to acquittal. They convert our eternal separation from God to eternal life in the glory of God's presence. God Himself takes the initiative and provides the means whereby we are removed from the realm of death to spiritual regeneration.

We who were objects of God's wrath because of our sin now become objects of God's mercy. Notice that God's mercy is described as a rich treasure, just as His grace and glory were in the first chapter (1:7, 18). His mercy is His compassionate action on behalf of those unable to help themselves. God is merciful in that He does not punish us as we deserve. God is infinitely merciful to the worst of sinners. His saving acts of mercy for us arise out of "His great love with which He loved us." God demonstrated His love for us when He sent His Son to die on the cross for our sins (Romans 5:8).

"Made us alive together with Christ" (v. 5)

Here Paul reveals the central idea of the long sentence that began in verse 1. But first he reiterates what he had stated there, that we were *dead* in trespasses and sins. Then he makes his great point, that even when we were in that hopeless and helpless condition, God "made us alive together with Christ." This means more than the simple fact that God has given us spiritual and eternal life in Christ. And it is more than a forecast of our future bodily resurrection. The key phrase is *together with Christ*. When Christ was raised, we were raised up together with Him to be victors over sin. When we fully grasp this truth, we can set our minds on things above and not on things on the earth; we will no longer be "alive" to the attractions of this world (Romans 6:5-14; Colossians 3:1-2).

In contemplating the saving work to take us from being dead in trespasses and sins to being made alive together with Christ, Paul pauses in his train of thought to exclaim, "by grace you have been saved" (v. 5). He has already mentioned *God's mercy* in saving us from judgment, and *God's love* in sending His Son to die for us (v. 4). It is as if he cannot restrain himself from also mentioning *God's grace* in making us alive with Christ. Grace gives to us what we never deserved and could never attain—new life in the risen Christ.

"Raised up together . . . sit together" (v. 6)

God not only made us alive with Christ as a work of His grace, He "raised us up together, and made us sit together in the heavenly places in Christ Jesus" (v. 6). The same expressions are used of the climax of the exaltation of the Lord Jesus Christ in chapter 1 (v. 20). The victorious Christ who has conquered His enemies is now ascended to heaven and seated in triumph at the Father's right hand, and we believers have been joined to Christ in His resurrection, in His ascension, and in His enthronement at the Father's right hand in "heavenly places"! His victory is our victory and His exaltation is our exaltation. We are to realize that we are no longer bound to this world. Our true position is in our Savior at the Father's right hand. Therefore we need not be overcome by the tensions, trials, and temptations we face in this present evil world. Our position with Christ is a most liberating truth.

A Display of the Riches of His Grace (v. 7)

The purpose of believers being made alive with Christ and exalted to the heavenly places in Him is "that in the ages to come He might show the exceeding riches of His grace." In the ages to come, God will demonstrate to the angelic hosts the glory of His grace by continuing to express it "in His kindness toward us in Christ Jesus." Angels never have, nor ever will, experience God's grace for themselves. But they will, however, glorify God for what they see Him doing for us, His redeemed people. God's redeeming grace is so broad, so deep, so high, and so great, that it will give us, too, opportunity to learn ever-widening themes of worship at His feet.

We should get rid of the idea, held by some uninformed believers, that our heavenly occupation will be little more than strumming harps while walking golden streets or looking up friends of earth for long conversations about the "old days"! The glory of heaven will be the Lord Jesus Christ, and the theme of heaven will be God's grace.

"By grace . . . through faith" (v. 8)

The believer's journey has taken us from God's wrath to God's glory, from death to life, from eternal judgment to eternal blessing. But how could we be cleared of the charges against us? How could we be delivered from the death that engulfed us? And how could we qualify for a place at God's right hand in the heavenlies? To answer these questions Paul summarizes here the dynamic truths of the gospel in crystal clear language: "For by grace you have been saved through faith." Grace is God's love and kindness working on behalf of those who are totally undeserving of any favor and totally helpless to remedy their plight. On His own initiative, and by His own power, God acted to save lost people at a tremendous cost to Himself. He gave His only Son to bear their punishment on the cross and become their Savior. By this act—entirely of His own doing—He provides atonement (satisfaction) for sin and is justified in clearing the charges of guilt against sinners.

Saving Faith

The question still remains as to how guilty people, unable to help themselves to any degree, can appropriate the benefits that come from God's grace. The answer is that they are saved "by faith" (belief) in God. As Paul told the jailer in Philippi: "Believe on the Lord Jesus Christ and you will be saved" (Acts 16:31). The faith or belief referred to is more than intellectual assent to Christian truth. A person exercises biblical, saving faith when he acknowledges his sin, confesses that Christ died on the cross as his substitute, and, in a one-time conscious act, personally receives, or embraces, the salvation from judgment that God offers (John 1:12; Romans 6:23). Note that the text says we "have been" saved, meaning that what was done on the cross has ongoing effectiveness. Nothing else will ever be required. Salvation is complete for eternity.

"The gift of God" (vv. 8b-9)

Paul qualifies what he has been saying with the words, "and that not of yourselves, it is the gift of God." Excellent commentators are divided as to whether the word "that" refers to the larger subject of salvation or to the faith we exercise in the gospel message. It is sufficient to say here that salvation by grace through faith is a gift from God and *no part of it* is generated by us. To make sure no one misunderstands, Paul states that salvation is "not of works, lest any man should boast." In other words, in case anyone should think about boasting of their works as deserving salvation. Since salvation's basis is in God's grace, no amount of religious activity, self-denial, generous giving, or compassionate service will contribute anything at all to it. If we could do something to earn our salvation, God would be put under obligation to us and we *would* have cause to boast (Romans 3:27).

"His workmanship" (v. 10)

While good works have nothing to do with how we are saved, they have everything to do with how saved people are to live. When we were saved by grace through faith we were made spiritually alive "according to the purpose of Him who works all things according to the counsel of His will" (1:11; 2:5). Part of that purpose is now stated: "we are His workmanship created in Christ Jesus for good works." The word *workmanship* refers to something that has been made. The Greeks used it to refer to works of art like statues, paintings, architecture, songs, or poems. When God made us alive in Christ He made us "works of art" that display the intention and skill of the divine Artist.

As His works of art we are "created in Christ Jesus." It is the second time we become the subject of His creation. First, in terms of our human existence, "all things were created through Him and for Him." Second, in terms of our spiritual life in Christ, we are a "new creation" (2 Corinthians 5:17). We are His works of art, His masterpieces. As an artist with a lump of clay, He is shaping us into the image of His Son and preparing us to be used for His glory. To do this He uses the tools of His Spirit, His Word, His servants, and ordained circumstances. As God's masterpiece, the life of a mature, godly believer is the most beautiful thing this side of heaven.

God has made us "for good works, which God prepared beforehand that we should walk in them." We do not work to be saved, but when we are saved we must work, for works are the fruit of faith and salvation. The works we are to do have been designed according to God's predetermined plan. Notice that they are designed "that we should walk [live] in them." It is therefore required of every believer to be "equipped for every good work" (2 Timothy 3:17), "zealous for good works" (Titus 2:14), and careful to "maintain good works" (Titus 3:14).

In conclusion, let us remember that our salvation story began when we were *spiritually dead* (vv. 1-3). We became *spiritually alive* in Christ and were seated with Christ in heavenly places (vv. 3-6). It came about by God's *amazing grace* as a gift to undeserving sinners (vv. 8-9). It is worked out as God's *wonderful masterpiece* in our lives as we do the good works that God has prepared for us (v. 10). The passage began with our "walk" as dead men unable to please God (vv. 1-2). It concludes with our "walk" as people made alive in Christ and able to accomplish what He has planned for us.

4

RECONCILIATION OF JEWS AND GENTILES THROUGH THE CROSS

Ephesians 2:11-22

Chapter 2 began with an explanation of salvation by grace through faith. In this section Paul takes another step forward to show us that saved Jews and Gentiles are, through Christ, not only reconciled to God but to each other. What both parties would have declared to be impossible, God accomplished through the blood of Christ by making them fellow citizens in God's household.

The Animosity between Jews and Gentiles (v. 11)

Writing to the Gentile believers in Ephesus, Paul reminds them of their relationship with Jews before they were saved. They were "Gentiles in the flesh." From God's perspective, there were two main people groups before the church was formed: Jews and Gentiles. The Jews thought of themselves as far superior to the Gentiles because God had called them to be a separate nation and a special people (Deuteronomy 7:6-7). They were proud of their prophets, their land, and their nation. They were proud of the fact that the Scriptures had been entrusted to Jewish authors and that the coming world ruler (the Messiah) was to be Jewish. They were so proud that they despised all other people—that is, Gentiles.

In addition to all the aforementioned privileges, God gave the Jews the rite of circumcision as a physical mark of their special relationship to Him.

But instead of being God's channel of blessing and an example to the surrounding nations they became a self-serving people and held the Gentiles in contempt. With this attitude they arrogantly called themselves the "Circumcision" and referred to the Gentiles as the "Uncircumcision" (v. 11). Over time, circumcision had become merely an external rite. Paul recognized this and adds his own disdain for their boasting by calling it "circumcision made in the flesh by hands," because what they were doing was only external. As such, it was unacceptable to God (Leviticus 26:41; Romans 2:28-29). True circumcision is "not made with hands" (Colossians 2:11) because it has to do with removing the influence of "the flesh" (our old nature). Paul used the terms "Circumcision" and "Uncircumcision" to highlight the enormous gulf between Jews and Gentiles.

The Alienation of the Gentiles (v. 12)

In reminding the Gentile Christians in Ephesus of their condition before they were saved, Paul mentions five things that had once characterized them in relation to their standing before God. The first was that they were "without Christ" (Messiah). They did not know about Him, nor could they claim any relationship to Him as the Jews could. The second was that they were "aliens from the commonwealth of Israel." They stood outside the realm of blessings that belonged to the descendants of Jacob. The third exclusion factor was that they were "strangers from the covenants of promise." God made covenants with Abraham, Isaac and Jacob, but He never put Himself under obligation to fulfill any promises to Gentile peoples (with the exception of the covenant he made after the flood via Noah in Genesis 9:8-17). Fourth, they had "no hope," because their false religions and false gods offered them none. Finally, they were "without God in the world"; they had to deal with the difficulties of life without God's help or blessing.

In summary, before they were saved, these Gentile believers were without Christ, without citizenship, without promise, without hope, and without God. On an individual basis, they had always had the opportunity to choose to believe in the one true God and become part of the covenant people, but most of them failed to do so. Their dilemma of complete alienation from God is the dilemma of the unsaved world today. Paul asked these Gentile converts to "remember" their former state so that they would better appreciate the wonder of God's grace that had transformed them.

Now Made Near (v. 13)

Against this background, the solution to the dilemma of Gentile alienation from God is now revealed. In sharp contrast to being "far off," these believers had been "made near" to God. Centuries earlier, the prophet Isaiah recorded that the Servant of the Lord would be God's "light to the Gentiles" and His salvation would reach "to the ends of the earth" (Isaiah 49:6). The blood of Christ shed on the cross accomplished the transition from "far off" to "near." Their sin separated them from God, but Jesus' death at Calvary (His "blood") had brought them near to God. In today's world, reference to the blood of Christ is offensive—even repulsive—to some, because of the implied violence. But the violence of the crucifixion and the shedding of His blood are essential elements in the saving work of Christ (1 Peter 1:18-19; 1 John 1:7; Revelation 1:5).

Christ is Our Peace (v. 14)

The blood of Christ removes the enormous barrier of sin between man and God. It enables us to enjoy peace with God. The sacrifice of Christ also removes barriers that separate man from man and allows us to enjoy peace with our fellow Christians. Paul now deals with this subject, especially in the relationship between Christian Jews and Christian Gentiles. He begins by stating clearly that Christ Himself is our peace. It is not simply that Christ mediated peace between Jews and Gentiles; He *is* the peace between them because they are united in Christ. Paul has used the phrase "in Christ" or "in Him" twelve times up to this point in Ephesians to indicate that believers, whether Jews or Gentiles when they were unsaved, are now in Christ as a single entity. Because they are both in Him, He is their peace, just as Micah predicted: "And this One shall be peace" (Micah 5:5).

The cessation of hostility between Jew and Gentile in the early church was one of the triumphs of grace. Christ "made both one." At the cross their old identities fell away and the only identity that mattered was their identity in Him. They were not to be identified as Jewish or Gentile any more. They had become an entirely new category of people who soon came to be known as "Christians," meaning they belonged to Christ (Acts 11:26). At the same time they also became part of a new entity, called the church of God (1 Corinthians 10:32).

The Wall of Division Between Jew and Gentile (v. 14)

Christ not only made both Jew and Gentile one entity; He also broke down "the middle wall of division" that existed between them because of their mutual hostility (v. 14). Most commentators think that Paul may have been thinking of one of the walls in the temple complex in Jerusalem as an illustration. This wall separated the inner courts (where only Jews were allowed) from the outer court (where Gentiles were permitted to observe the ceremonial worship of the Jews, and to which they were confined).

The ancient historian Josephus wrote of inscriptions on this wall forbidding Gentiles to proceed further on pain of death. Two of these inscriptions, called the *Thanatos* (Greek for "death") *inscriptions,* have actually been found and are on display in museums in Jerusalem and Istanbul. The wall in the temple area, with its inscriptions, illustrates the non-material "wall of division" of which Paul speaks in this chapter. Possibly Paul was remembering his own experience about four years prior to writing this letter. At that time some Jews sought to kill Paul just because they believed (mistakenly) that Paul had brought a Gentile Christian named Trophimus into the forbidden Jewish area of the temple in Jerusalem (Acts 21:27-31).

The Demolition of the Wall (vv. 15-18)

1. He Abolished the Ceremonial Law (v. 15)

The wall was broken down by the work of Christ on the cross. Paul discusses several aspects of how this came about. Through His death, Christ abolished the enmity (state of war) that existed between the Jews and the Gentiles by doing away with "the law of commandments contained in ordinances," that is, ceremonies. This phrase refers to the Old Testament laws of the Jews that regulated their religious duties and symbolized the spiritual work of the coming Messiah. They were the instructions about the feasts, sacrifices, priesthood, cleanliness, clothing, etc. All these were only for Jews, and as such they embodied the differences between Jews and Gentiles. Under those laws, Jews could neither eat with Gentiles nor worship God with them.

When Christ died "in His flesh" on the cross, these ceremonial ordinances were abolished. Neither Jews nor Gentiles needed the temple any longer, nor did they need the many laws concerning the feasts, the priesthood, or the sacrificial system. Believers from Jewish and Gentile backgrounds are both "in Christ." Nothing separates them. We should keep in mind that while the "ceremonial law" was abolished, the "moral law" of God, as summarized in the Ten Commandments, was not abolished. It reflects the holy character of God and does not change. The Lord Jesus Christ said He did not come to destroy the law (Matthew 5:17-19) but to fulfill it, which He did, perfectly.

2. He Created a New Humanity (v. 15)

The next thing Christ did to break down the "wall" was to create one "new man" or humanity. This is more than simply being united to Him and therefore to each other. Christ created in Himself "one new man from the two," something entirely different from what had ever existed before. The "new man" refers to the church, in which there is neither Jew nor Gentile (Galatians 6:15). The result of the creation of the church is expressed in the words, "thus making peace" (v. 15). This is the biblical answer to all prejudice and racism among the people of God. It needs to be diligently recognized and demonstrated in every community of redeemed people.

3. He Made Reconciliation through the Cross (v. 16)

The third thing Christ did was to "reconcile them both to God . . . through the cross." Note that this reconciliation was more significant than the reconciliation of the two groups to each other. The emphasis here is that they were *both* reconciled *to God*. Both groups had become estranged from God through their sin. The great need of both was reconciliation to Him. The Lord Jesus provided the answer "through the cross." It was where God "reconciled us to Himself through Christ" (2 Corinthians 5:18-19). As a result, when forgiven Jews and forgiven Gentiles met at the cross, the age-old enmity between them was put to death.

4. He Preached Peace (v. 17)

When Christ broke down the wall between Jew and Gentile He brought the good news of peace. We learned that He *is* our peace (v. 14), and that He *made* peace through the cross (v. 15). Here Paul borrows language from Isaiah, who prophesied of one who "proclaims peace . . . who proclaims salvation." Isaiah also recorded God pronouncing, "Peace, peace to him who is far off and to him who is near" (Isaiah 52:7; 57:19). Because Christ made peace at the cross, He preached peace after He rose from the dead. On resurrection day, His first words to His disciples were "Peace be with you" and "Peace to you" (John 20:19-21). He continued to speak through the apostles, who preached peace to both the Gentiles who were "afar off" and to the Jews who were "near." The word *preach* means to "announce," "proclaim," especially good news, which in this context is the "gospel." The word is often used in the New Testament with respect to evangelizing, preaching the gospel of salvation. The work of the early Christians, like ours today, was to preach peace through Jesus Christ (Acts 10:36).

5. He Gave Access to the Father (v. 18)

The final thing Christ did in breaking down the "wall" was to give believing Jews and Gentiles free and unlimited access to God as *Father*. Under the old covenant, access to God was limited. People worshipped and prayed to Him as Creator God, as the Covenant-keeping God (*Yahweh*), and as Master (*Adonai*), but they did not know or address Him as Father. The Jewish High Priest was restricted to a once-a-year access into the Holy of Holies in the tabernacle (and subsequently the temple) for the purpose of atoning for the nation's sins, not for prayer. All other Jews were kept at a distance, and Gentiles had to become proselyte Jews even to join them. Christ opened the way for all believing Jews and Gentiles to have the privilege of immediate access to the presence of the Father.

These wonderful truths should stimulate our prayer when we understand that every member of the Godhead is active every time the humblest believer approaches God as "Father." We pray to the Father, through the Son, with the help of the Spirit.

Images of the Church (vv. 19-22)

The final verses of this chapter illustrate some of the wonderful privileges of those Gentiles who had become part of the church, the new humanity. Before being saved, their relationships with God and His people had been described as "uncircumcision" (v. 11), "aliens" (v. 12), "strangers" (v. 12), "afar off" (v. 17), and "foreigners" (v. 19). When they became believers, God gave them new and wonderful relationships with Him and other believers. Three striking images illustrate these relationships: citizenship in a city, membership in a family, and stones in a temple.

"Fellow citizens with the saints" (v. 19)

This final section in chapter 2 begins with "Now, therefore," indicating something new in contrast to the past: they now enjoyed privileged status in contrast to estrangement from God. To illustrate the new status, Paul uses the imagery of citizenship in a Roman city. To be a citizen of a Roman city was a highly prized privilege. Acts 22:28 indicates that it could be bought "with a large sum" of money (Acts 22:28), and people who immigrate to the United States spend years qualifying to become citizens, but becoming a citizen in God's "city" was immediate, free, and of far superior value than Roman or United States citizenship. As "fellow citizens with the saints" they could rest in the knowledge that they were first-class citizens of God's international community of believers known as the church. Psalm 16:3 defines saints as "excellent ones" in whom God takes delight. Both believing Jews and believing Gentiles now comprise that company.

"Members of the household of God" (v. 19)

A second illustration of the Gentile believers' new relationship to God was their (and our) membership in God's household. We are children in God's family. In chapter 1 we learned that we were adopted as adult sons so that we can enter into many privileges (1:5). Previously in this chapter we have learned that we can pray to Him as Father (2:18). In this verse we are all part of God's household, whether Jews or Gentiles. We are *brethren* in His family. *Brethren* is the most commonly used term for believers in the New Testament. In God's family we accept one another as brothers and sisters. We support and help one another and enjoy one another's company.

Stones in God's Temple (v. 20)

Paul goes into greater detail in describing the relationship of believers to the church with his third image, that of a temple.

1. The Foundation

The church as a temple is "built on the foundation of the apostles and prophets." The apostles are the disciples of Jesus, and this includes Paul and a few others. The prophets are mentioned after the apostles and most probably refer to New Testament prophets who were the Spirit-inspired teachers of the early church. Some became the inspired authors of the

New Testament (Mark, Luke, Jude, and James). What they taught was "the apostles' doctrine" (Acts 2:42).

Commentators wrestle with what Paul meant by "foundation." Were the apostles and prophets *themselves* the foundation, or was *their teaching* the foundation? It seems best to understand that the foundation of the church is the teaching of those who were either eyewitnesses of Christ Himself or the recipients of divine revelation (3:5). Their teaching was the body of truth concerning Christ that is now contained in the New Testament Scriptures. From the Day of Pentecost onward, these teachings called the "apostles' doctrine" have been the foundational truths on which the church was built. The church stands true to God's purpose in Christ because it stands firmly on this foundation.

2. The Cornerstone (vv. 20-21)

The chief cornerstone of the church is Jesus Christ. Cornerstones on public buildings (such as Herod's temple) were large precut stones which were placed on one corner of the foundation, thus determining the exact position and the architectural unity of the building. The other stones were aligned horizontally and vertically to the cornerstone to ensure the integrity of the building. The Greek word for cornerstone can also refer to the keystone of an arch or the capstone of a pyramid, both of which may have symbolic meaning. The Jerusalem temple, however, was a block shaped building with heavy stone walls. Its cornerstone would have been laid first on the foundation. From it, all the other stones would have been joined and aligned. This is the more likely model of Christ, the chief Cornerstone. Whichever of the models may be in view, the basic truth symbolized is that Christ is the most important stone in the entire building.

The prophet Isaiah spoke of the Messiah (Christ) as "a precious cornerstone, a sure foundation" (Isaiah 28:16). Paul taught the Corinthian believers of Christ the foundation (1 Corinthians 3:11). Here in Ephesians he builds on Christ's role as the Cornerstone, "in whom the whole building, being joined together, grows into a holy temple in the Lord" (v. 21). Thus the building will have unity, being "joined together," and it will have life, for it "grows." Peter said that believers are "living stones . . . being built up a spiritual house" (1 Peter 2:5). The building will also have purpose, for it becomes "a holy temple in the Lord."

Where God Dwells

Paul then turns from his illustration to apply it to "you also," the Gentile believers in Ephesus, who were a local expression of the church of God worldwide. As such they were "being built together for a habitation of God in the Spirit" (v. 22). In a similar vein, he said to the Corinthians, "You are the temple of God" (1 Corinthians 3:16). The temple in Jerusalem was built by Solomon to be the dwelling place of God among His people. When it was complete and the Ark of the Covenant was brought into it, the glory-cloud of God's presence filled the place (1 Kings 8:6-12). God's awesome visible presence there illustrates His spiritual presence in the spiritual temple of the church. The church as the assembly of believers is His dwelling place on earth. Both Jewish and Gentile believers share in the wonderful privilege. As we understand these images and the privilege of these relationships we have with God and with one another as citizens, family members, and stones in a temple, we should humbly bow in worship.

CHAPTER

5

THE MYSTERY OF THE CHURCH

Ephesians 3:1-13

In light of the significance of the truths of chapters 1 and 2, Paul now wants to pray for the Ephesian believers that they would realize the enormous implications of these truths. He introduces his prayer by reminding them of his present situation in relation to them; he was "the prisoner of Christ Jesus for you Gentiles." He had been a prisoner of Rome for about five years since his arrest on false charges in Jerusalem (cf. Acts 21:24). Prior to that, he had been imprisoned in Caesarea for two years where he had hearings before Governors Felix and Festus and before King Agrippa. The King would have released him, but Paul appealed to Caesar in Rome, which was where he was at this time, awaiting trial (Acts 21-28).

A Prisoner of Christ Jesus (v. 1)

Five years is a long time, but Paul did not blame either the Jews for accusing him or the Romans for imprisoning him. Paul had the perspective that he was in prison as "the prisoner of Christ Jesus." Being in prison was merely the present sphere of his service for the risen Lord. Two of the ways that he served there were in witnessing to others around him and in writing four letters that have become part of Holy Scripture. Another perspective Paul had was that he was a prisoner "for [the sake of] you Gentiles." His life's ministry had been to reach Gentiles. His current imprisonment was because he had declared to the Jews that God had sent him to Gentiles (Acts 22:21-22). Thus he could say to the Gentile believers in Ephesus that he was a "prisoner of Christ Jesus," specifically for the sake of "you Gentiles."

At this point in his writing, Paul seems to become overwhelmed by the fact that God had used him to reveal God's grace to them and that God had given them many privileges that flowed from His grace. He expands on these thoughts and does not return to his prayer until verse 14 where he repeats the phrase "For this reason" to reintroduce it.

"The dispensation of the grace of God" (v. 2)

Paul was confident they were aware that God had given him a special responsibility in relation to "the dispensation of the grace of God." The "if" in verse 2 can be translated "since." The word "dispensation" here refers to the administration of a trust. The word can be used of a *personal stewardship,* such as the one given by God to Paul that he might pass on truth to believers (Colossians 1:25). Here, though, its sense is *a divine administration*, where God manages His affairs with man in specific ways during a specific period of time. The term "dispensation of the grace of God," as used in this passage, refers to God's current administration of His grace regarding salvation through Christ (Ephesians 1:10; 3:2, 9).

In the previous dispensation, God established Israel as the chosen nation through which He communicated to man. From the time of Moses, Gentiles could be saved and could worship God by becoming Jewish proselytes. That was the former administration, sometimes called *the dispensation of law*. When Christ rose from the dead and the church was formed by God's grace, composed of both Jews and Gentiles, the new administration was called *the dispensation of the grace of God*. The dispensation of grace will be followed by another called the *dispensation of the fullness of the times* (1:10).

A Mystery Revealed (v. 3-4)

The truth about the dispensation of the grace of God is called "the mystery" and "the mystery of Christ." We noted in the comment on Ephesians 1:9 that Paul uses this word "mystery" to describe a truth previously unknown but now revealed. He wants the Ephesian believers to understand that the truth concerning God's grace came to him by direct revelation from God— when or how, we are not told. When Paul says that he had previously written about the mystery, it may refer to what Paul wrote in Ephesians 2:14-22, or perhaps to what he had just written to the church in Colossae, a letter that was carried by Tychicus along with this one to the Ephesians (Colossians 1:24-25).

The Explanation of the Mystery (vv. 5-6)

The crux of the mystery is that the church is made up of both Gentiles and Jews who had been saved and brought into union with Christ *and* with one another. It was a truth completely unknown in previous ages. Paul told them that God had now revealed it "by the Spirit to His holy apostles and prophets" (v. 5), that is, New Testament apostles and prophets (2:19-20). The Old Testament prophets who lived in "other ages" had no understanding of the church as it is revealed in the New Testament. There is no direct teaching about the church anywhere in the Old Testament. Paul declares emphatically that the mystery concerning the church was "*hidden from ages* and from generations, but has *now has been revealed* to His saints" (Colossians 1:26, emphasis added). It was by His Holy Spirit that God revealed this truth to Paul and other New Testament apostles and prophets, and by them to all the saints (vv. 3, 5).

Israel and the Church are Different

It is important that Bible students carefully differentiate between Israel and the church. Stephen's reference to Israel as "the congregation in the wilderness" (Acts 7:38) is no argument for the case that God views the church as having replaced Israel for future blessing and purpose. The Greek word for both church and congregation is used for almost any type of assembly in the New Testament, from a heathen mob (Acts 19:32) to a local church (1 Thessalonians 1:1). Paul, James, and John all used the word to refer to both the universal church and local churches.

In Old Testament times, God chose His earthly people, Israel, to be the instrument of His blessing to the world. In New Testament times, Israel's role was set aside until Christ comes again. In this current age, God has made His heavenly people, the church, to be His means of blessing to the world. This was a difficult concept for the Ephesians to grasp, and for this reason Paul repeats it several times in the first three chapters. Even the apostle Peter struggled to accept the truth that believing Gentiles were equal with Jews under the new order (See Acts 10).

Three Shared Privileges (v. 6)

Paul explains the mystery by declaring that it contains three remarkable privileges for the Gentile converts that they share equally with Jewish converts (v. 6). These three privileges have been mentioned previously in Ephesians.

Here he gathers them together. The first is that believing Gentiles and believing Jews are *heirs together* to enjoy all the blessings God has for His family (1:11, 14, 18). The second is that they are *members together* of the same body (1:22-23; 1 Corinthians 12:12-13). Every Gentile member of His body is equally important with every Jewish member, and all members are necessary for its complete functioning. A third privilege is that they are *partakers together* of God's promise in Christ in relation to the gospel. Both believing Jews and believing Gentiles share in the many promises that the gospel comprises, just two of which are the permanent, the indwelling of the Holy Spirit in each believer and eternal life with the glorified Christ.

The Minister of the Mystery (vv. 7-9)

Paul's focus now moves from explaining what the mystery is to rejoicing in his own calling as a minister of the mystery. Some Christians use the word *minister* to refer to an ordained preacher in a church, but in the New Testament it is simply the common word for a servant. It emphasizes duty and responsibility rather than status or position. Paul did not make himself a minister. God called him to His service from the day he was saved (Acts 26:16). As a servant of the gospel he was given the mystery as a gift of God's grace and was both entrusted to proclaim it and enabled to proclaim it (v. 7a). It was by God's mighty power that Paul, the self-righteous Pharisee, was saved and given special revelation of the mystery of grace, made a servant of the gospel, and called to this ministry (v. 7b). He was conscious of God's daily enabling grace.

The ministry of the mystery to which Paul was called was truly wonderful. But he did not want his readers to think that because God had called him to this important role he was anyone special. He expresses surprise and modesty that God would reveal it to him at all. He said he was "less than the least of all the saints" (v. 8). This humble attitude was typical of Paul. In his letter to the Corinthians he called himself "the least of the apostles" (1 Corinthians 15:9), and to Timothy he said he was the "chief" of sinners (1 Timothy 1:15). This was not false humility, nor was it morbid self-depreciation. Paul was conscious of his own unworthiness and the wonder of God's grace in allowing him to serve in this way. His humility, far from being a detriment to his usefulness to God, was the key to it. There is a powerful lesson here for every servant of God today who wants to be used in His service.

Once again Paul states that God's grace was given to him so that he could preach to the Gentiles (v. 8; Acts 9:15; 22:21; 26:17; Galatians 1:16). He termed the subject of his preaching/evangelism to Gentiles, "the unsearchable riches of Christ." In this context the riches refer to the mystery that God's marvelous grace should be poured out upon Gentiles. In Ephesians 2:7 these riches were shown to be "exceeding." Here they are "unsearchable" because they can never be fully explored. They can be linked with the riches of His goodness, forbearance, and longsuffering (Romans 2:4); with the riches of His wisdom and knowledge (Romans 11:33); and with the riches of His glory (Ephesians 3:16). All these riches have made every true believer a spiritual billionaire.

The Fellowship of the Mystery (v. 9)

Another reason why God's grace was given to Paul was "to make all people see what is the fellowship of the mystery." The phrase "make all people see" is literally to *enlighten* or *bring to light* those who were in darkness. The commission Jesus gave to him when He first called him on the road to Damascus was to go to the Gentiles "to open their eyes and to turn them from darkness to light" (Acts 26:17-18). The word *fellowship* is the same word rendered *dispensation* or *administration* in most versions, which are to be preferred (cf. v. 2). This dispensation had once been "hidden in God." He had created it just as He had created the universe and everything in it and now was making it known through Paul and his fellow apostles and prophets to all people.

The Mystery Revealed to Angels (vv. 10-11)

God intended not only that "all people" be enlightened about the unity of Jew and Gentile in the church, but also that "principalities and powers in heavenly places" learn the manifold wisdom of God through the church. God's "manifold" wisdom means "the richly diversified nature" of God's wisdom. People from every tribe and nation on earth have become part of the great new community of grace. The church is God's masterpiece which He displays to these heavenly dignitaries to teach them about the multifaceted, or variegated, wisdom of God. The result of their observation is that they glorify God in line with the great eternal purpose of all God does. In a coming day, redeemed people will join the angels in heavenly praise (Revelation 4:8-11; 5:8-14; 19:1-7).

As angelic beings observe the church and God's ongoing dealings with it in grace, they learn what they did not know before. They learn that Satan's purposes were frustrated and that God's purposes were completed in triumph over evil and for the salvation of believers. They learn that those who had offended God were now reconciled through the victory of the cross. Not only that, but those reconciled were also blessed with all spiritual blessings and enthroned with Christ in heavenly places. They learn that the Jews and Gentiles, indeed the entire multi-cultural community in Christ, is united in one body. More than that, angels learn that God receives more glory as a result of Christ's redeeming work and the formation of the church than He would have if sin had never entered into the world. No doubt the demons look on in horror as the evil designs of Satan are frustrated. At the same time the angels watch in wonder to see what God has done and bow down in worship when they comprehend it (Hebrews 1:6).

One of God's purposes in designing the church is to demonstrate His multifaceted wisdom to the whole angelic realm. When believers understand that the angels are observing them, they should take special care how they act. Paul told the women of Corinth that when they prayed or prophesied they were to have a symbol of authority on their heads "because of the angels" (1 Corinthians 11:10). He charged Timothy to maintain discipline in the church before God and the Lord Jesus Christ and the "elect angels" (1 Timothy 5:21). Angels, who have long desired to look into the meaning of the suffering and glory of Christ, pay close attention to how the members of Christ's body are living and worshipping (1 Peter 1:10-12). We should be aware that the behavior of believers is important because angels observe it as they carry out their ministry to us (Hebrews 1:14).

The Eternal Purpose (v. 11)

It was God's eternal purpose to redeem people from slavery to sin, to reconcile them to Himself, and to form them into a spiritual body, the church, with His Son as the head. God planned all this before the foundation of the world. His Son accomplished it through His incarnation, death, resurrection, ascension, and enthronement, and so it is called "the mystery of Christ." Every new believer is incorporated into the church, the body of Christ. When we grasp this truth we should, with the angels, bow down and worship.

Praying with Confidence (vv. 12-13)

We have already learned that those who have peace with God the Father also have access to Him in prayer through Christ by the Spirit (2:17-18). Now, Paul encourages us to use our access to God in prayer with boldness and full confidence (v. 12). We have immediate access into the presence of God in prayer at any time and under any circumstances. We need no human priest, no saint, not even Mary the mother of Jesus, as an intermediary. We enter God's presence freely because we are now accepted "in Christ." Nothing else is needed. We can certainly come to Him with confident assurance when we approach Him in prayer. "Let us therefore come boldly to the throne of grace that we may obtain mercy and grace to help in time of need" (Hebrews 4:16).

Concluding this section, Paul encourages his Ephesian readers to enter into his personal perspective on his sufferings and to "not lose heart" (v. 13). It seems that they were grieving over his long imprisonment and the pain and suffering caused by it. They should see instead that his suffering was a divinely-ordained part of his ministry. He was suffering for their benefit because he was obeying the will of God. He was a prisoner for their sake (v. 1) and they needed to understand that the outcome was their own glory, or future eternal blessing. Paul leaves us a worthy example here of maintaining an eternal perspective on suffering for Christ's sake.

6

PAUL'S PRAYER FOR POWER AND LOVE

Ephesians 3:14-21

This passage is Paul's second great prayer for the Ephesian believers. He had begun to report his prayer for them with the words "For this reason" in verse 1, followed by the statement to the saved Gentiles that he was a prisoner for their sake. Then he digressed from his prayer to more fully explain the truth of the mystery that, in Christ, God had made Gentiles coheirs with believing Jews. Although this truth had prompted his imprisonment, Paul told the Ephesians to have a broader view of God's purposes so that they should not lose heart on his account (vv. 2-13). Now he tells them how he was praying for them, repeating the same expression, "For this reason" (vv. 1, 14). His prayer is based on the truth that the new humanity, the church, was a temple where God dwelled (2:21-22). His prayer begins with an introduction (vv. 14-15). It ends with a doxology giving glory to God for His limitless ability to demonstrate His power in us (vv. 20-21). Between these it focuses on three primary requests (vv. 16-19): for power, for knowledge, and for fullness.

The Introduction to Paul's Prayer (vv. 14-15)

With great reverence Paul begins, "I bow my knees to the Father." He echoes the words of the psalmist, "Oh come, let us worship and bow down; let us kneel before the Lord our Maker" (Psalm 95:6). In bowing his knees, he shows his *humility and submission* as he acknowledges the greatness of God the Father. In bowing down Paul also shows his *passion and concern* in prayer as their spiritual mentor. Five years, before he had said goodbye with tears to the elders of this very church. He pleaded with them to guard the sheep of the local church and to watch out for the "wolves" who were bent on its destruction. In that moment of passionate concern he "knelt down and prayed with them" (Acts 20:36). The Lord Jesus too, in the intensity of His emotion at Gethsemane, "knelt down and prayed" (Luke 22:41). Kneeling in prayer is a posture of humble submission to God and passionate concern for the request. How beautiful when believers show these attitudes by kneeling in prayer.

Paul prays to "the Father of our Lord Jesus Christ" (cf. 1:2-3). He had already mentioned the freedom of access we have to the Father through Christ (2:18). Now he begins his prayer for the believers by linking it with the intimate relationship between God the Son and God the Father. The Lord Jesus had addressed God as Father in the most crucial moments of His life. We hear Him pray as He leaves the Upper Room, "Father, the hour has come" (John 17:1). We hear Him again on His knees in Gethsemane saying, "Father, . . . not My will but Yours be done" (Luke 22:42). And on the cross He prays, "Father, forgive them" and "Father, into Your hands I commend My spirit" (Luke 23:34, 46).

The Father is described as the One "from whom the whole family in heaven and earth is named" (v. 15). The original of "whole family" probably means that all believing people, both in heaven and on earth, claim His fatherhood. They are the ones who truly derive their names from God the Father. Another translation has "every family," which would include the groupings of angelic beings in heaven and of human beings on earth. A third translation has "all fatherhood," which would refer to fatherhood in its broadest sense.

The Prayer for Power (vv. 16-17a)

The first request in the prayer is that the Ephesian believers would be "strengthened with might through His Spirit in the inner man." God's power was fully available to strengthen them spiritually. The power was to come through the exceeding generosity of God who gives "according to the riches of His glory," that is, corresponding to the riches of His glory (cf. Philippians 4:19).

As we make use of the blessings and riches we have in Christ that Paul has described in the letter thus far we become strong in our convictions, settled in our assurance, and established in the great truths of salvation, which include forgiveness, redemption, and coming glory. God strengthens us with might by His Spirit when He leads us into the full appreciation of all these truths concerning Christ. The calm assurance that the Holy Spirit brings through the Word puts us in a place of strength when false teaching occurs, when doubts arise, when our faith is challenged, and when obedience is needed. It is worth noting that it was not until the Holy Spirit came upon the disciples that they had power to evangelize the world (Acts 1:8).

Power in the Inner Man

Note that our strength is to be in the sphere of the "inner man." It is what we term the heart, the part of our being in which we have personal consciousness, emotional responses, and the will to make moral choices. As we feed on the Living Word and as the Spirit of God takes the Word of God and applies it to our lives, we are made strong. This does not happen overnight, but our spiritual endurance grows as we partake of spiritual food and face daily challenges with spiritual responses and decisions. This strength is not to be some elevated experience of an elite few. It is to be the experience of every Christian, as it was for Paul. As he grew older in the work of the Lord and the battle scars began to multiply, he sensed that though the "outward man" was perishing, yet "the *inward man* is being renewed day by day" (2 Corinthians 4:16, emphasis added).

The tragedy is that so few of God's people experience spiritual victory in the struggle against sin in the inner man or in spiritual power in their walk with God. Spiritual strength will be evident, not so much in public service, but in our constant, trusting communion with God, no matter the outward circumstances. If Paul were alive today he would pray the same prayer for us.

Christ Dwelling in our Hearts (v. 17)

Parallel to his request that the Ephesians be spiritually strong, Paul prays that Christ would dwell in their hearts by faith (v. 17). Factually, Christ is present in every believer, but experientially our passage teaches that the more we become like Him, the more He can "dwell" or settle down in our hearts. It is the Spirit who enables us to be more like Christ (2 Corinthians 3:18). The more like Christ we become, the more "at home" He is in our hearts. Jesus told the disciples that if they loved Him, He and His Father would come to make their "home" with them (John 14:23). When Christ is at home in our hearts, we become conscious of His presence in every aspect of our lives. He becomes the focus of our lives, we allow Him full control, and we welcome His direction in everything. He rules at the center of our personalities including our minds, wills, and emotions. Paul prays that the Ephesians would grasp the truth and *believe* that the second Person of the Trinity wanted to "dwell" in their hearts.

A Prayer for Knowledge

Paul's prayer for knowledge in verse 19 is made in the context of the believers "being rooted and grounded in love." He uses two metaphors to describe the state they were either in or needed to be in to be able to have that knowledge. One metaphor is related to crops on the farm and the other to buildings in the city. On the farm, plants are to be well rooted; in the town, the buildings are to be firmly founded.

The Soil and the Foundation (v. 17b)

In the first metaphor, love is the soil in which they, the plants, are rooted. Just as soil provides moisture, nutrients and stability to the plant, so love provides growth and stability to the believer. A healthy plant that is well rooted will fulfill its intended purpose and will be able to withstand wind and storm. The branches and leaves can do their work of absorbing light and producing fruit as food for others. When believers are firmly rooted in love they will produce spiritual fruit (cf. Galatians 5:22-23). In the second metaphor, love is the foundation of a building. Love is the base on which the relationships of believers are founded. Just as a building with a solid foundation protects and provides for the welfare of the people using it, so believers who have a firm foundation in love can protect and provide for the whole fellowship.

When we are rooted in love we grow spiritually strong and bear spiritual fruit. When we are founded in love we stand firm and provide for the fellowship, prayer, worship, and service of the community of believers. Both the soil and the foundation are love. The love of which Paul speaks always gives unselfishly for the good of others. It is an act of the will, not a feeling. It is a reflection of the love of the Father who gave His Son to save us. It also reflects the love of the Son who gave Himself for us. When we are rooted and grounded in this love we are in a position to be able to comprehend the dimensions of Christ's love as explained below.

Comprehending Love's Dimensions (v. 18)

Paul has prayed that we might be strengthened by the power of the Spirit, indwelt by the conscious presence of Christ, and established in love. His next request (for knowledge) is presented in a corporate way: "with all the saints." It is a request that can only be grasped when it is considered, studied, discussed, and shared with other believers. It is so all-encompassing that no single person can fully take it in. To know His love we must share our growing enjoyment of it with each other. Paul begins by praying that we might have the power to grasp four dimensions: width, length, depth, and height. The text does not specifically say what the dimensions refer to. It does go on to add another request—that we may know the love of Christ. Scholars have wrestled with identifying the object of the four dimensions and what its relationship may be to the "love of Christ" in verse 19.

Within the parameters of this study it is enough to say that the majority view is that the four dimensions refer to Christ's love, though it is not specifically stated. This conclusion is based on several reasons. First, that the four dimensions are described as one large unity by the use of the definite article "the" that governs them all. The four-dimensional unity can be understood as referring to the next clause, "the love of Christ," with which it is closely connected. Second, the word "comprehend" in verse 18 is parallel to the word "know" in verse 19. Third, in his letter to the Roman believers, Paul has previously referred to two of the dimensions, height and depth, in connection with the love of Christ (Romans 8:37-39). If Paul was connecting the dimensions to Christ's love, then the essence of his prayer is that believers would be able to understand the love of Christ more fully.

Four Dimensions of Christ's Love

The four dimensions are a literary expression that describes Christ's love as infinite, surpassing, and beyond comprehension. In keeping with the theme of Ephesians, four aspects of love can be seen in relation to the mystery of Christ. His love is so wide that it includes those who were aliens and strangers (2:12). It is so long that it reaches from eternity past when we were chosen in Christ to eternity future when the riches of His grace will be explained (1:4; 2:7). It is so deep that it brought Christ down from the glory of heaven to reach us who were dead in trespasses and sins (2:1). It is so high that we have been raised up together and made to sit together in heavenly places (2:6).

There is a paradox here when Paul prays that we *know* Christ's love that *surpasses knowledge*. But the more we grow spiritually, the more we are enabled to grasp some of love's limitless dimensions expressed in the redeeming work of God's Son. This is not intellectual knowledge about which one may write an essay. Rather, it is the life-changing knowledge of His love that leads us to worship Him reverently, to serve Him gladly, to find victory over adversity, and to endure hardship to the end. Love is the world's most powerful force.

Fullness of God (v. 19)

Paul's final request is that we may be filled with the fullness of God. This relates to our experience rather than our position as members of the church, through which we already participate in His fullness. In a practical sense we are to strive to possess more and more of His fullness in a growing daily relationship with Him.

There is an ongoing tension between what we are in Christ and what we are to become; between our present state of fullness and our continuing growth in fullness. To be filled with God implies we should be emptied of self. We should constantly yield to the Holy Spirit's working in us to change us into the image of Christ. Paul's prayer is that this transformation to spiritual maturity will result in believers being filled to the measure of all the fullness of God. Only when we are with Christ and like Christ will this be fully realized. David said it like this: "I shall be satisfied when I awake in Your likeness" (Psalm 17:15). It is the kind of fullness found in the final prayer of the Lord Jesus when He prays that the love with which the Father loved Him would be in them (John 17:26).

God's Limitless Ability (vv. 20-21)

Is God able to answer huge requests like these? The final two verses give us a clear answer in a doxology, or hymn of praise, that is closely connected with the prayer. Paul now brings his prayer to a conclusion in which he praises God's super-abounding ability to give us those things and greater things that we cannot even imagine. A doxology always gives the worshipper reasons to glorify God, and this one is no exception.

The first reason why we should glorify God is that He is all-powerful; He is "able." The second reason we should glorify God is that this limitless power "works in us." It is not theoretical power, but actual power. It not only exceeds our ability to understand; it is also available. It is the same power that raised Christ from the dead (1:19-20). And the wonder of this power is that it works in us as well as in the apostle. We believers are included in the thinking and the asking, as well as being recipients of the power. With this limitless resource available, believers can fulfill God's purpose in them.

"To Him be glory in the church" (v. 21)

Paul ascribed glory to our great God "in the church." The church is God's masterpiece through which He is displaying His wisdom to the spiritual powers. And when the church is complete it will become the glorious bride of the Lamb who will display His glory. God's glory is also seen "in Christ Jesus" (a preferable reading to "by Christ Jesus"), who is the focus of God's glory. The duration of the glory is to continue "throughout all ages, world without end."

With this doxology, the doctrinal part of Ephesians comes to a conclusion, having shown God's wonderful salvation effected through Christ and the inclusion of both Jew and Gentile in one entity, the church. The great doctrinal truths have been applied in two wonderful prayers that the believers might be empowered to understand God's mighty purposes as they are worked out in them.

WALKING IN UNITY

Ephesians 4:1-16

The Theme of Walking

Beginning with chapter 4, the second half of Ephesians explains how the truths unfolded in the first three chapters were to be lived out in the Ephesian believers' lives. The word Paul uses to describe this practical Christian living is "walk." He has already used it to describe their lives before they were saved when they "walked" in "trespasses and sins" (2:1-2). He used it again concerning the "good works" in which they were to "walk" after they were saved (2:10). Walking is a common New Testament metaphor of Christian living. In Romans 6:4 Paul instructs those who were saved and baptized to "walk in newness of life." He told the Thessalonians how they ought to walk and please God (1 Thessalonians 4:9-10). The apostle John commanded the believers to "walk just as He [Christ] walked" (1 John 2:6). Walking, in these passages, describes believers going in the right direction, to the right destination, in the right manner, and making constant progress.

In chapters 4 and 5 Paul uses the word "walk" five more times to teach us how to conduct ourselves as believers (4:1, 17; 5:2, 8, 15). These five references speak of our walk in unity, in holiness, in love, in light, and in wisdom. In the first three chapters believers are described as *seated* with Christ in the heavenlies. In chapters 4 and 5 we are described as *walking* with Christ in our daily lives. While we walk on earth we are to reflect the character of our risen life with Christ in the heavenlies.

Therefore . . .

The passage begins with the hinge-word "therefore," indicating the transition from knowing the truth to living it. It is similar to the "therefore" in Romans 12:1, which opens the practical part of that book. The Christian walk, as described in the last three chapters of this book, is our logical response when we grasp the Christian calling in the first three chapters. We are obligated by the truth to live up to its standards.

Walking Worthy of Their Calling (v. 1)

Paul starts by reminding his readers that he was a "prisoner of the Lord" (cf. 3:1), that is, a prisoner of Christ. Chained as he was to Roman guards, and bearing in mind what it was costing *him* to walk with the Lord, he led into his teaching on walking worthy of their calling. Negative circumstances do not change our obligation to live for the Lord. Notice also that he *entreated* them, he pleaded with them to walk in a way consistent with their calling (cf. Romans 12:1). Their calling was designed by God in eternity past. It was accomplished by God's redeeming grace and power. They appropriated it by faith in Christ. It resulted in Jews and Gentiles being reconciled to form a new entity called the church. The church is God's masterpiece, displayed to the universe and centered in God's Son. On the basis of the sublime truths associated with this calling, Paul pleads with them to walk in a manner worthy of it.

Characteristics of a Worthy Walk (v. 2)

The way in which we can walk worthy of our high calling is to exhibit four primary graces in relation to other believers. These graces are lowliness, gentleness, longsuffering, and loving forbearance. We are to cultivate these graces because all of them are necessary to reach the goal of unity mentioned in the next verse. All four are characteristics of the Lord Jesus Christ. They are also part of the fruit of the Spirit (Galatians 5:22-23). The first two belong together, and the second two belong together. Jesus told the disciples to walk in step with Him because He was "gentle [meek] and lowly [humble] in heart" (Matthew 11:29). These characteristics were despised by the culture of the Greco/Roman world, just as they are by our modern world. But they are the hallmark of true Christian character. The Lord of glory was silent in meekness before His accusers and submissive in humility to those who condemned and crucified Him. We who walk in His steps must also be both gentle and humble in a world where these values are ridiculed.

The third grace in a worthy walk is longsuffering, or patience. We need it when we are provoked by other people and their shortcomings. With patience we can harness our tempers for the sake of unity with our spiritual family. The final grace is "bearing with one another in love." Our love for others who are in Christ shows itself in our enduring faults in their characters, personalities, and temperaments (1 Corinthians 13:7). Longsuffering goes beyond common courtesy, which may not be motivated by love at all. It is to bear with others, genuinely loving them, even when they irritate and annoy us.

The Unity of the Spirit (v. 3)

In addition to the four graces, their worthy walk must include the endeavor to keep the unity of the Spirit. The language here indicates a sense of urgency. They were to diligently strive to "keep" a unity that had already been provided by God's Spirit (1 Corinthians 12:13). He has united every believer to every other believer. Jesus prayed for this unity in His High Priestly Prayer (John 17:11, 23). It is, therefore, our continuing priority to maintain the unity of the Spirit among believers.

The unity of the Spirit is to be preserved "in the bond of peace." Peace can be likened to the ligaments that hold our human bodies together. Peace holds God's people together when they are united, when they are of "one accord and of one mind" (Philippians 2:2). But only people who are humble, meek, patient, loving, and forbearing will be able to have the mind of Christ and thus be able to maintain peace in the church. How needed this is in a world where divisions within and between churches abound. Disunity is perhaps the saddest factor in Christendom today.

The Uniqueness of Our Faith (vv. 4-6)

There are seven elements unique to the Christian faith. First there is *one body*, which is the body of Christ, the church. Paul has already written of it to them (1:23; 2:16). Into this body, believers of all categories have been incorporated. Christians should resist every effort that breaks down the oneness of the body. The second unique element in Christianity is the *one Spirit,* the Holy Spirit, who created the church on the Day of Pentecost.

He dwells in every believer and brings unity to the whole body. The third of these elements is *one hope of our calling.* This is the destiny to which God has called us by His grace. In the time of the consummation of all things we will be with Him and like Him. The final verse of an old hymn goes,

> "Then we shall be where we would be,
> Then we shall be what we should be;
> Things that are not now nor could be
> Soon shall be our own."

> — Thomas Kelly

"One Lord, one faith, one baptism" (v. 5)

Another unique element of the Christian faith is that there is *one Lord* (v. 4). He is the "one Lord Jesus Christ through whom are all things, and through whom we live" (1 Corinthians 8:6). In the polytheistic world of the first century, as well as in our pluralistic world today, it is vital to affirm that we have one unique Lord. Fifth, there is *one faith.* This refers to the body of truth which was "once for all delivered to the saints" (Jude 3). It is contained in the Word of God, particularly in the New Testament, and is to be believed by all God's people. There can be only one faith because there is only one Lord. There cannot be multiple truths or multiple ways to heaven. Jesus said, "I am the way. . . . No one comes to the Father except through Me" (John 14:6).

Sixth, there is *one baptism.* This has been interpreted as either our baptism by the Spirit into the body of Christ (1 Corinthians 12:13) or water baptism as a symbolic expression of faith in Christ and union with Christ (Acts 2:41). The Ephesian believers would probably think of their own water baptism when they read this (Acts 19:5). They had acknowledged "one Lord," embraced "one faith," and testified to their salvation by being immersed in water as a public expression of their faith. The emphasis here is that all the Jews and the Gentiles who had been saved in Ephesus had been baptized. Water baptism is, or should be, for every believer, a church ordinance that is obeyed.

"One God and Father of all" (v. 6)

The seventh unique element to our Christian faith is that there is "one God and Father of all who is above all, and through all, and in you all" (v. 6). The Old Testament only occasionally refers to God as Father. The context of Malachi 2:10 is that God is Father in the sense of being the creator of the human race, but in the New Testament God is commonly referred to as the Father of all believers. He is "above all," referring to His universal rule and transcendence over everything. He is "through all," referring to His ability to use everything to bring His purposes to pass. And He is "in you all," referring to His presence within believers. It should also be noted that the Trinity is prominent in this list of unique elements: there is one Spirit, one Lord, and one Father.

Christ's Gifts to the Church (vv. 7-12)

After describing the unity of the church as a body, Paul now tells of the great diversity among its members. The theme in these verses is the occasion of Christ giving gifts to all the members of the body. We can use these gifts to accomplish the goal of unity because we have been given "grace," or spiritual enablement, to do so. A particular gift is given to each member "according to the measure of Christ's gift." He measures out the gift (the spiritual capacity) to every member of the body, and He measures out the grace (the spiritual enablement) to use it for His glory. The gifts are entirely His choice, not ours. The same gifts are also spoken of as gifts given by the Spirit (Romans 12:4-6; 1 Corinthians 12:8-11). There is no contradiction here, for the Spirit Himself was given to the church by the exalted Christ.

Paul references Psalm 68, which is a victory psalm written by David to celebrate the capture of Jerusalem and the subsequent bringing of the Ark of the Covenant to Zion. He summarizes or quotes loosely from verse 18 to show that in ascending to the city in triumph, the enemy was defeated and gifts were distributed. David's triumphant ascent to Jerusalem and distribution of gifts pictures the ascension of Christ after His victory at the cross. He ascended to the glory of heaven leading a victory parade of those He has released from the power of sin and Satan (Hebrews 2:15). At the end of the column were the defeated enemies, now His captives: Satan, sin, and death. Thus Scripture says, "When He ascended on high, He led captivity captive," or perhaps better, "He led captive a host of captives" (NASB). Then to the cheering crowds he distributed gifts to mark the celebration. This verse pictures Christ as the exalted Victor giving gifts to the church.

Ascended Above the Heavens (vv. 9-10)

Paul includes a parenthesis to comment on the ascension of Christ mentioned in verse 8. Before He could ascend He had to descend "into the lower parts of the earth," also translated as "the earth below" or "lower earthly regions." This phrase, referring to Christ's descent, has been understood in three ways. It may refer to:

- ✓ His descent into Hades between His death and resurrection.

- ✓ His incarnation when He came to earth and was conceived in Mary's womb.

- ✓ His entire life and work on earth, beginning with His incarnation and including His life ministry and His ultimate humiliation in death and burial as a prelude to His ascension.

The third of these views best fits the context. Christ "came down from heaven" to earth in His incarnation (John 3:13). He lived on earth "taking the form of a servant" (Philippians 2:7). He humbled Himself, descending to the lowest depths of humiliation, "even the death of the cross" (Philippians 2:8).

This qualified Him to be exalted, and He rose from the grave in triumph over His foes. He ascended to the right hand of His Father (1:20; 2:6). He assumed His place "far above all the heavens that He might fill all things" as the Ruler on the throne of the universe and as "head over all things to the church" (v. 10; 1:22). Thus, from His suffering and death He ascended in triumph to fill all in all (1:23). In particular, He fills the church by giving it gifts as explained in the next two verses.

Christ's Gifts to the Church (vv. 11-12)

After establishing Christ's authority to give gifts to the church, Paul names several significant gifts, but to our surprise they are not *spiritual abilities* given to individual believers as mentioned in verse 7 (cf. Romans 12:6-8, 1 Corinthians 12:1-11); instead, they are *specially gifted people*, honored men given to the church at large for the equipping of others to serve and for the growth of the whole church (v. 12). Notice that all of these gifts are communicators of the Word of God. The apostles and prophets received the Word, the evangelists preach the Word, and the pastors and teachers share and teach the Word.

The first category of gifted men is called *apostles*. In this context, apostles were the leading men chosen by Christ for the purpose of establishing the church and making disciples (Matthew 28:18-19; Acts 1:8). One way they qualified was to have witnessed Him being alive from the dead (Acts 1:22). To confirm their status they performed signs and wonders (2 Corinthians 12:12; Hebrews 2:4). The eleven disciples and Paul met these qualifications (Paul having seen a vision of Christ on the road to Damascus). The second specially gifted group were *prophets*—people who speak for God. Prophets received revelation from God and communicated it to others. Both apostles and prophets were associated with the "foundation" of the church (2:20). When the apostles who had seen the risen Christ were dead and some of the prophets (as well as some of the apostles) had finished giving us the New Testament Scriptures, the need for these two foundational "gifts" was over. There are no apostles and prophets of this nature in the church today.

The next group of men given to the church is *evangelists*. These are especially gifted to preach the good news of salvation to unsaved people. All believers are to evangelize, but these are equipped to be the pioneer missionaries and church planters. Philip and Timothy are the New Testament examples (Acts 8:40; 2 Timothy 4:5). Today, evangelists would be sent out from a "home" church to accomplish their calling. *Pastors* are shepherds and their work has to do with the care, guidance, and protection of the flock. They encourage the sheep, restore them when they go astray, and warn them of surrounding dangers. Every biblical local church has multiple shepherds, also called elders and overseers (Acts 20:17, 28; 1 Peter 5:1-2). Those shepherds mentioned here for the larger body could be likened to conference speakers and writers today.

The final men-gifts in this list are *teachers*. Such men are gifts from God enabled by Him to explain the Word of God clearly and to apply it to believers' lives. Many commentators understand "pastor / teachers" as one combined gift, not two. This cannot be established with any certainty. The two gifts often function together, but just as often they function separately. God has powerfully used gifted teachers and shepherds to build up the body of Christ down through the centuries.

The Purpose of the Gifts (v. 12)

Exclusive leadership belongs to Christ. These specially gifted men listed above are neither to function as the head of the church nor maintain a monopoly on the church's ministry. Our text indicates that these gifts have a threefold purpose—to equip, to serve, and to edify (build up) the body. It is helpful to see these three purposes as a series of steps. These men equip the saints; the saints serve the body; the body is built up. To put it in another way: by their teaching and shepherding the gifted men equip the saints *so that* the saints may serve *with the result that* the body of Christ grows. Thus believers themselves are equipped to build the body; they should not leave the job to leaders. Church growth, then, is to be stimulated by gifted people and carried out by all believers. Nowhere in the New Testament is there a clergy / laity distinction as is so commonly practiced today.

The Aims of the Growing Church (v. 13)

In verse 13 Paul presents another "big picture" of the church in terms of time and its maturity. The process of church growth through the ministry of well-equipped believers who build up the body will continue until we come to a state of unity, maturity, and conformity. The first of these ("the unity of the faith and the knowledge of the Son of God") is corporate agreement of Christian doctrine as it applies to our lives and thinking and corporate knowledge of Christ. This state will finally be brought about when Christ takes the church home, at which time all our differences of opinion will dissolve into full agreement at His feet. In this, as in so many things, there will always be a tension between the "already" and the "not yet," but godly people will constantly strive for unity in doctrine.

The second state to which we are coming is maturity in spiritual development. The "perfect man" is the mature Christian community that emerges from the proper use of spiritual gifts. The mature church is one that functions the way it was designed to do: as a body of members who fulfill their functions under the control of Christ, the head (v. 16).

The third state to which the church is coming is "the measure of the stature of the fullness of Christ." We aim to be a full-grown, unified body which complements our glorious head. We have not "arrived" until this is true. Thus it will only be realized when the church is complete with Him in heaven. As we look forward to that coming day we should be motivated to constantly be growing in unity of the faith, in maturity, and in conformity to the Lord Jesus Christ.

Dangers of Immaturity (v. 14)

In light of the glory of full maturity, Paul warns his readers not to be "children," babies in terms of spiritual development. He uses five striking word pictures in this verse to describe the dangers of immaturity. They were to be careful so that they would not be:

✓ "tossed to and fro" by false teaching, like a drifting boat in the waves.

✓ "carried about" by false doctrine, like blowing clouds in the wind.

✓ gullible to "trickery," like a novice at a gambling table.

✓ victims of "cunning craftiness," like an unwary business person.

✓ caught out like an unwary traveler, robbed by bandits who "lie in wait."

Growing Up into Christ (v. 15)

Instead of losing their grasp on truth through immaturity they were to hold the truth in love. "Holding" is the marginal reading for the word "speaking" in our text, and is preferred by many commentators. It is imperative that spiritually-equipped believers in a united and growing local church maintain the truth, especially of the gospel. We not only speak it; we must also defend and explain it. When we meet people who disagree with us we should remember to hold the truth with love. All our dealings with others should reflect that love. In so doing we will grow up "into Christ," that is, become more like Him in every aspect of our lives. Whether we are talking about the church as a whole or individually, Christ is the measure of our Christian development. As our head, He has all authority, and we are to yield to His control in everything. In this way it is "no longer I who live, but Christ lives in me" (Galatians 2:20).

Growth Is from Christ (v. 16)

The growth of the whole body is empowered by Christ: He "causes growth of the body for the edification of itself in love." By His design, every member of the body is to function in unity exactly as He directs. As an illustration, think of your left forefinger pressing on a violin string in exactly the right place and time with the right pressure. That happens only as your arteries bring fresh blood and your veins carry depleted blood away. Your finger joint flexes correctly as tendons are tightened by muscles in the arm and as nerves bring feeling to the fingertip. All these functions are coordinated by the head. Each one of them is important and must perform correctly to press one string for one moment to produce the correct sound for one instant. Imagine how many such functions are required to play one line of one hymn!

The coordination required for the effective working of the members of the body of Christ is even more intricate than that required for playing the violin. Thus every Christian has an important part to play in both the local church and in the larger body of Christ worldwide.

8

WALKING IN HOLINESS

Ephesians 4:17-32

In the first half of chapter 4, Paul appeals to the Ephesian believers to *walk in unity* as members of the body of Christ. In this second section, Paul appeals to them to *walk in holiness,* that is, in a new lifestyle that reflects the holy and righteous character of God (vv. 17-32). Harmony in the church is to be complemented by personal holiness. He pleads with them not to fall back into their pre-Christian ways of thinking and behavior. They must abandon their former pagan lifestyle, "as the rest of the Gentiles walk" (cf. 1 Thessalonians 4:5), and embrace the new lifestyle as members of the "one new man" (2:15).

The Gentile Walk Described (vv. 17-19)

To press home the contrast between the old and the new, Paul describes in graphic language the lifestyle of pagan Gentiles in that day which these believers were being urged to completely abandon. It will be evident to the reader that the pagan lifestyle of that day is similar to the lifestyle of millions in ours. Observe, too, the similarities between this description and that in Romans 1:18-32. Their new lifestyle was to be marked by holiness, which means to be "set apart."

1. Their Thinking was Futile (v. 17)

In this context, futility means empty and without any purpose, chasing after shadows. Our natural minds invent plausible ideas that are empty of truth and are thus dangerous. Moral judgments start in the mind, and because the mind is depraved, if its conclusions do not take God into account they are intellectually futile (Romans 1:21, 28). Futile thinking is, by definition, pointless; it accomplishes nothing of any lasting value.

2.   Their Understanding was Darkened (v. 18)

In similar language, Paul told the Roman Christians, "Their foolish hearts were darkened. Professing to be wise, they became fools" (Romans 1:21-22). In 2 Corinthians 4:4, unbelievers are said to be "blinded" by Satan. John 3:19 characterizes them as men who "loved darkness rather than light, because their deeds were evil."

3.   They were Alienated from God (v. 18)

In rejecting the light of God's revelation of His attributes in nature they went farther and farther away from God, becoming increasingly ignorant of Him. He gave them over to their chosen pathway (Romans 1:24-28). Their willful determination or stubborn hardness of heart made them unresponsive to truth.

4.   Their Morality was Calloused (v. 19)

They gave themselves to sensuality. In doing so they lost their capacity to feel shame. They no longer had any sense of the consequences of sin. They were determined to gratify self at all costs and constantly lusted for more forms of immorality. How clearly their actions reflect the moral callousness of our generation!

The School of Christ (vv. 20-21)

After describing their pre-conversion thinking as dark, alienated, ignorant, and hardened, Paul contrasts what they had learned since conversion. He says, "But you have not so learned Christ." He goes on to describe their progress in Christian thinking using the imagery of a school. Note the educational verbs such as "learn," "heard," and "taught." Christ was the subject they had been taught. Christ was also their Teacher, because when He ascended He gave gifts of spiritual teachers through whom He taught the church. Some of these gifted men taught the Ephesian converts. In saying that "the truth is in *Jesus*," Paul is probably drawing their attention to how the Lord modeled the truth in His life on earth. His words, actions, and reactions were reported by the early teachers and now recorded for us in the four Gospels.

Today, we have the complete Word of God that includes the Gospels. We, too, should measure ourselves by the standard of His life and teachings as one way to hinder slipping back into former ungodly lifestyles.

Take Off the Old Clothes (v. 22)

Paul moves on to exhort the Ephesians to put off, or discard, their "former conduct" or old way of life as pagans. All that they were before their conversion is described as the "old man" or old self. The old self is corrupt and morally degenerate. It cannot be renewed or improved. It gives in to deceitful desires that satisfy the flesh and strangle the soul. Paul describes the old self and its way of life as being like a filthy old garment that needs to be taken off and replaced by new clothes.

The command here to "put off . . . the old man" should be seen together with other statements in Scripture on the subject. In the context of teaching about believer's baptism (which pictures our union with Christ in death), Romans 6:6 explains that our "old man" was crucified with Him (Romans 6:4), having been condemned at the cross by God (Romans 8:3). In Colossians 3:9 we read that when we died with Christ we put off "the old man with his deeds." Spiritually, all believers are now with Christ in the heavenly places and the old man has been put to death.

In the light of what is already true spiritually, we are exhorted to make it true practically by *reckoning* on the death of our old man and thus putting away the sins of the old life (Romans 6:11). As long as we live, there will always be a tension between *our perfect standing* in the heavenlies with Christ and *our imperfect state* on earth. All the sins that characterized the old life are to be put off in disciplining ourselves to walk worthy of our calling. For all of us there are relationships, entertainments, activities, and thoughts that are the clothes of the "old man" needing to be deliberately "put off."

"Be renewed in the spirit of your mind" (v. 23)

Instead of living the old way of life we are to be renewed in the spirit of our mind (v. 23). Paul challenged the Roman Christians to be "transformed by the renewing of [their] mind" (Romans 12:2). The "spirit" of our mind refers to the "inner person," where the direction and motivation of our thinking is formed. It is in this sphere that the renewing work is done. The word "spirit" in verse 23 does not refer to the Holy Spirit; it is the spirit *of* our mind, not *in* our mind. Notice that the verb ("be renewed") is passive. We do not renew our minds ourselves; rather, we must allow the Holy Spirit to do this, accomplishing in a practical, ongoing way what He sets in place at conversion (Titus 3:5). It is He who transforms us into the image of Christ one step at a time. Our role is to yield ourselves to Him (2 Corinthians 3:18). With renewed minds we view the world and its temptations in an entirely new light.

Put on the New Clothes (v. 24)

What we are to be actively and deliberately doing is putting on "the new man." Just as the "old man" is all that we were in Adam, so the "new man," or new self, is all that we are in Christ. Old things have passed away and all things have become new, in the sense of different (2 Corinthians 5:17). The parallel passage in Colossians 3:8-14 is worthy of close study. Just as we turned away from the old life, so we are to turn toward and embrace the new life. In this way we become partakers of the divine nature (2 Peter 1:4). The transformation takes place when we read and meditate on God's Word and communicate with God in prayer. By these disciplines, God's Spirit renews our minds and brings our wills into conformity with God's.

Our new man is made in "righteousness and true holiness" when we are created in the likeness of God (at salvation). Righteousness is to do right and holiness is to live apart from sin. One way we can understand the two concepts together is to see holiness as our duties to God, which are reflected in the first four of the Ten Commandments (Exodus 20:3-11) and right-eousness as our right acts toward people, which can be seen in the last six Commandments. Recognizing what we are in Christ, we are to put off the old clothes of the old life and put on the new clothes of the new life.

Exhortations to Change (vv. 25-5:2)

Paul gives attention now to five specific ways in which the believer can put off the old man and put on the new. They are commands and each has a negative and a positive side. Negatively, we are to stop committing the offending sin. But that is not enough. Positively, we are to replace the offending sin with a righteous act.

1. The Change from Falsehood to Truth (v. 25)

"Therefore," based on the principle of replacing the sins of the old self with the graces of the new, Paul exhorts, "Putting away lying, each one speak truth with his neighbor." Truth is a good starting point in the light of the statement that "the truth is in Jesus" (v. 21). Lying is perhaps the most common sin of all. It is found everywhere: in politics, business, the media, religion, home life, and relationships. It is found in many forms such as cheating, exaggeration, flattery, deception, withholding information, and giving false information. Lying began in the Garden of Eden when Satan, the father of lies, deceived Eve. The believer is to "put away" all lying and replace it with speaking truth.

Truth should characterize everything we do because Christ is the truth, the Holy Spirit is the Spirit of truth, and God's Word is truth (John 14:6, 17; 17:17). We are to actively speak truth because the person to whom we speak is our "neighbor" whom we are to love. Within the church our relationships are even closer because we are closer than neighbors; we are "members of one another." Thus our speech should always be reliable, honest, and sincere. Strong relationships are dependent on trust that in turn is dependent on truth. Speaking the truth does not mean that we must always tell everyone everything they want to know. There are times when we should exercise strict confidence or discernment—saying what is appropriate or relevant. When we do speak the truth, we should do so in love (cf. v. 15). Truth about negative things should not be used as a weapon to hurt someone else.

2. The Change from Unrighteous Anger to Righteous Anger (vv. 26-27)

The next change from the old man to the new man is in the cause and the care of anger as an emotion. The command is "Be angry, and do not sin." The phrase is taken from Psalm 4:4 and has to do with the danger of anger being mixed with sin. Anger *at* sin is a godly emotion. The Bible portrays God as righteously angry with His people and with the nations (2 Kings 17:18; Zechariah 1:15). Because God is righteous, He is angry at sin everyday (Psalm 7:11). The Lord Jesus was angry with the Pharisees because they wanted to prevent His healing the man with the withered hand on the Sabbath (Mark 3:5). He was also angry with the money-changers who were misusing the temple for their own profit (Matthew 21:12). For the believer, righteous anger is a legitimate response when either God or people whom we love are injured by the sinful acts of others.

Sinful anger is anger that is self-serving, vindictive, and undisciplined. It is to be put off. Even righteous anger, when allowed to simmer, can turn into resentment and self-righteousness. For this reason we are told to "not let the sun go down" upon our wrath. Vindication is entirely God's business, and whether the anger is righteous or unrighteous we are not to let it continue. By dwelling on it, we are giving the devil an opportunity to tempt us to take vengeance (2 Corinthians 2:11). The Lord said, "Do not avenge yourselves, but rather give place to wrath" (Romans 12:19).

3. The Change from Stealing to Sharing (v. 28)

The third change in lifestyle for the new believer is from stealing to sharing. Evidently Paul had in mind some converts who had been in the habit of stealing before they were saved. This had to stop. Like lying and vindictive anger, this sin is rampant everywhere. There are many ways in which we can steal, and they are all offensive to God. Theft from loved ones at home, from the workplace (in time or materials), from the tax collector, from employees by underpayment—these are all examples.

The alternative is to "give to him who has need." Hands that used to take what did not belong to them must now be occupied by useful labor. Paul worked diligently with his own hands and exhorted the Thessalonians to use theirs (1 Corinthians 4:12; 1 Thessalonians 4:11). Paul had reminded the Ephesian elders a few years before that "these hands have provided for my necessities and for those who were with me" (Acts 20:34). In the same passage he went on to say that "by laboring like this" they must support the weak because the Lord Jesus had said, "It is more blessed to give than to receive" (v. 35). Thus, the believer who now no longer steals is to work hard at "what is good." He is to honor God by being honorably employed. He should also work with a view to sharing with others who have less than he does. In this way Christ changes the selfish thief into a generous Christian.

4. The Change from Corrupt Speech to Edifying Speech (vv. 30-31)

The next item of old "clothing" that needs to be exchanged for new is corrupt speech. The word *corrupt* is a word that describes rotten fruit or meat. Corrupt communication indicates everything that is rotten in the speech of the old man. It includes dirty and suggestive language, gossip, profanity, vulgarity, innuendo, or anything that does not reflect the character of God or build up the church. We need a guard over our mouths every day (Psalm 141:3).

We are to speak what is good for "necessary edification"; this brings help and blessing to the hearers. Our speech should be constructive, edifying, and uplifting. It should be gracious itself and appropriate to the hearer's need (Colossians 4:6). The Lord Jesus is the example of Christian speaking: "They marveled at His gracious words which proceeded out of His mouth" (Luke 4:22).

We are motivated to speak graciously by acknowledging the danger of grieving the Holy Spirit of God. Any type of corrupt speech or careless talk that falls short of the standard of God's holiness will grieve the indwelling Spirit. This verse supports the doctrine that the Holy Spirit is a person (although unseen), in that He has feelings and can be offended. And since He is the One who has sealed us until the day our bodies are redeemed (at the rapture), how could we even think of grieving Him?

5.   The Change from Evil Speaking to Forgiveness (v. 31-32)

The last item of old "clothing" that Paul exhorts the believers to exchange for new is a list of six sins. These are ways the "old man" in us reacts when we are the *objects* of "corrupt communication"—when people hurt us with their words. *Bitterness* means growing resentment or grudge. *Wrath* means passionate rage and is associated with *anger,* which is linked with hostility. *Clamor* is the excitement of a serious quarrel. *Slander* is defaming the character of another. *Malice* is the ill will that underlies evil schemes. Every one of these vices is to be completely eliminated from the Christian community.

When other Christians hurt us by what they say or do we are to respond to them with kindness, tenderheartedness, and forgiveness (v. 32). To be *kind* is to have a generous and gracious disposition like that of God who showed kindness toward us by saving us (Titus 3:4-5). We are to show kindness to those who do not deserve it. To be *tenderhearted* is to be compassionate toward those who offend us. To be *forgiving* is to be like God who forgave us when we could not pay our enormous debt of sin. The Greek word used here for *forgive* means to treat the offending person favorably and graciously. It's an action that flows from a generous attitude.

This attitude is well illustrated by the parable of the two debtors (Matthew 18:21-35). In that parable, the king "was moved with compassion" (v. 27) for the first slave and forgave him his debt. That slave did not show compassion to the slave who owed *him* money. Instead, he treated him harshly and "would not" (v. 30) forgive him his debt. Our attitude to those who sin against us should be like the king's. Christians should be eager to forgive the very moment that another Christian wrongs them.

CHAPTER

9

WALKING IN LOVE

Ephesians 5:1-7

Imitators of God (v. 1)

The exhortations that Paul gives believers in chapter 4 about living "worthy of our calling" continue in this chapter. In fact, the first verse completes the thought in 4:32 where we are told to be kind, tenderhearted, and forgiving "just as God in Christ has forgiven you." Paul says we are "therefore" to imitate God's generous disposition to forgive, which flows from His love and grace.

It is because we are God's dearly loved children that we are to respond in this way to those who offend us. The apostle John said, "Behold, what manner of love the Father has bestowed on us that we should be called children of God!" (1 John 3:1). In God's family we experience His love as He provides, encourages, protects, disciplines, and forgives. Just as children imitate their parents, so we are to imitate the forgiving nature of God toward those who sin against us. When Christ taught His disciples to forgive not just seven times for the same sin, but seventy times seven (Matthew 18:22), He was telling them to show compassion without limit to those who offended them. We can only do that when we grasp something of the extent to which God went when He gave His Son to die for us. And we can only do *that* when we grasp something of the extent of our offence against God for which we have been forgiven (cf. Luke 11:36).

Walking in Love (v. 2)

Walking in love is the third of the "walk" exhortations in the book of Ephesians (cf. 4:1, 17) Walking indicates progress in Christian living. Walking

77

in love is progress in the activity of compassion for others. When we walk in love we make progress in giving of ourselves for their good. The biblical concept of love is that which gives itself for the sake of its object. Christ so loved us that He has "given Himself for us." This means that in His act of love He handed Himself over as "an offering and a sacrifice to God" (cf. Galatians 2:20). The same verb is used negatively in the last chapter to describe how the unsaved Gentiles had "given themselves over to licentiousness" (4:19). It is also used to indicate the act of betrayal, which is the handing over of a friend to an enemy. Christian love that imitates Christ will result in giving ourselves up so that others may benefit.

The *model* of Christ's love was that He gave Himself for the sake of others. The *extent* of His love was that He gave Himself to the point of His own death on the cross. The cross is the ultimate demonstration of costly sacrificial love for undeserving people. The *wonder* of His love is that unworthy sinners are its beneficiaries. Here, again, our hearts should rise up in worship of our wonderful Savior.

"An offering and a sacrifice" (v. 2)

Christ's love is described as an offering and a sacrifice. An offering is something given to God. A sacrifice is an offering that is not only given to God but dies in being given. In the Old Testament, worshippers brought offerings to the temple such as grain and wine. They also brought sacrifices—selected animals and birds that were given and then killed and burned on the altar. Both offerings and sacrifices were expressions of the worshipper's praise, thanksgiving, and devotion as he or she approached God. Together they picture Christ giving Himself to do God's will and to become a sacrifice for our sin so that we could be forgiven. Christ as an offering and Christ as a sacrifice picture the way in which we are to give ourselves as an offering and a sacrifice for the benefit of others.

"A sweet-smelling savor" (v. 2)

Christ gave Himself as a sacrifice for a "sweet-smelling," fragrant aroma. We can easily picture the smoke from the burning sacrifices and offerings on the altar ascending to the sky. The aroma came from the burning sacrifice as well as from the offerings of grain with the wine that had been poured over them. As the smoke drifted upward, the worshippers discerned in the imagery that God was pleased with the offering. They understood that, symbolically, God smelled a sweet aroma in the smoke because the sacrifice was both pleasing and acceptable to Him.

The picture is twofold. First, it pictures the worshipper *bringing* his offering to the priests who offered it on the altar. Second, it pictures God *receiving* the offering, pictured by His "smelling" the smoke ascending into the sky. For both the worshipper and for God it was the quality of the sacrifice that was important. When the worshipper brought the right offering in the right way with the right attitude, it was acceptable to God. The smoke was to Him a *fragrant* aroma.

Of the five major offerings in Levitical times, the first three were described as "sweet fragrance offerings." The burnt offering illustrated Christ's total devotion to God (Leviticus 1). The grain offering depicted Christ's perfection (Leviticus 2). The peace offering illustrated Christ as Peacemaker between God and man (Leviticus 3). The other two offerings, the sin offering and the guilt offering, were not sweet fragrance offerings, because what they pictured was repulsive to God (Leviticus 4-5). They illustrated Christ bearing away our sins when He became sin for us (2 Corinthians 5:21). It was when He felt abandoned by His Father, when He bore our griefs and carried our sorrows, and when God laid on Him the iniquity of us all. It was when Jesus cried, "My God, my God why have You forsaken Me?" that God caused darkness to fall over the whole land for three terrible hours (Luke 23:44).

None of the sacrifices of the Old Testament were ever able to take away sins, even though they were repeatedly offered day after day for many hundreds of years. They were only shadows of the coming true Sacrifice. But now, "this Man, after He had offered one sacrifice for sins forever, sat down at the right hand of God" (Hebrews 10:12). He rose from the dead because His work was accepted by God the Father. Though His crucifixion was repulsive to the Father, once it was complete it became a "sweet-smelling aroma," acceptable and well-pleasing to God. This is why the apostle can comment here that God was pleased with the fragrance of His sacrifice.

The teaching for us here is twofold. First, we worship in wonder and amazement at His sacrifice that became a sweet-smelling aroma to God. Second, we learn that when we give ourselves for others by self-denying sacrifice, it too pleases God and is pictured as a sweet aroma to God.

The Perversion of Love (v. 3)

Paul contrasts the sacrificial love that was modeled by Christ and accepted by God with the selfish, counterfeit love that is worldly and devilish. What the world calls love is really lust. God's <u>agape</u> love is unselfish, forgiving, and pure, while Satan's counterfeit love is selfish, lustful, and impure. Instead of giving itself to meet the legitimate needs of others, counterfeit love focuses only on what satisfies itself. In doing this it fulfills its own perverted sense of need. It wants to give little and to get much in return. Jesus exposed it when He said, "If you love those who love you, what reward have you? Do not even the tax collectors do the same?" (Matthew 5:46). The world's quest for love is misguided and destructive because it is greedy and seeks only satisfaction. In the end, even the satisfaction of impure love turns out to be empty.

Paul now mentions several forms of counterfeit love of which we are to beware. They are all in the area of sexuality. *Fornication*, as used in this context, means any form of immorality outside the marriage of a man and a woman. *Uncleanness* includes anything unclean and filthy that appeals to our senses in the realm of sexuality. For us today it will be pornographic images and obscene language. These unclean things begin in man's imagination and are spread through the printed page, television, the internet, and interpersonal conversation. For the Christian all of it is unclean. None of it can ever be classified as anything but sin in the eyes of a holy God. There is no place for it in the life of a believer.

The Cookie Jar Syndrome

The next form of counterfeit love is *covetousness,* which in this context is lust or greed for more sexual satisfaction. Almost every addict to sexual sin talks of his or her insatiable desire for more. We easily fall into this trap by practicing what some preachers call the "cookie jar syndrome." The story is told that Johnnie's mother had just placed a fresh batch of cookies in the cookie jar. No one was to touch them until after dinner. When she heard the jar move she called out, "Johnnie, what are you doing?" He called back, "My hand is in the cookie jar resisting temptation." The cookie jars of our morally corrupt culture are everywhere inviting us to taste their wares. The challenge for us as Christians is to keep our hands out of the cookie jar.

Because sexual sins are especially powerful, Christians need to be exceedingly wary of the many traps that are snaring believers. Little by little we can easily adopt the standards of the world around us. The world considers sexual freedom to be a beautiful and legitimate expression of self. The marriage of a man and a woman is indeed beautiful, but every other form of sexual conduct belongs to the old life and should not even be named among believers (v. 3). God's people must eradicate sensual talk from their conversations. This includes inappropriate jokes, suggestive stories, and sexual innuendo. As "saints," we are set apart *for* God and set apart *from* sin.

Sexual sin is not only a sin of our modern times. The city of Ephesus was the religious capital of the cult of the Greek goddess Diana, or Artemis. Its enormous temple was one of the seven wonders of the ancient world. It was devoted to the worship of Artemis which was practiced openly on temple grounds in both male and female prostitution. Even in the commercial parts of Ephesus, prostitution was rampant. Still surviving among the ruins are chiseled out signs along the main street pointing people to the brothels. Ancient Pompeii, which was destroyed in a single day by the eruption of Mt. Vesuvius in AD 79, has been unearthed, and some of what is on view today gives evidence of gross pornography in its culture.

Sins Related to Sexual Impurity (v. 4)

Paul is not yet finished with his list of moral sins. He touches three more connected with spoken communication: filthiness, foolish talking, and coarse jesting. *Filthiness*s is general obscenity and is translated "shameful" in verse 12. *Foolish talk* in the Greek is related to our English word, "moron." It could be termed "gutter language." *Coarse jesting* is suggestive language with sexual innuendo. Christians often excuse it or laugh with it. But God's Word is clear—there is no place for it in the life of a believer.

Instead of using our speech for all this unprofitable language the believer is to give thanks with his lips. Thankful people understand that the goodness of God is everywhere and are quick to give Him thanks for every evidence of it. Even in the middle of terrible trials there are always things for which they can give thanks. If believers are known for anything, it ought to be that they love God and are unceasingly thankful. The command is definite: "In everything give thanks" (1 Thessalonians 5:18).

The Certainty of Consequences for Sin (vv. 5-6)

At this point, Paul reminds the Ephesians that there will come a time when God will no longer tolerate sin. God will punish people who practice the sins mentioned in verse 3—sins that should not even be named and are not fitting for saints. Now in verse 5 he mentions those three same sins again—fornication, uncleanness, and covetousness. People whose lives are marked by these sins demonstrate that they do not belong to Christ and have no inheritance in the kingdom of God.

The kingdom, as used here, refers to the sphere where the king rules. The subjects of the kingdom of Christ and God include believers in this age, in the millennium, and in the eternal state of glory. The meaning is that neither now nor in the future is there any place under God's rule for a godless lifestyle. God's grace has brought salvation and instructs us to deny ungodliness and to live "soberly, righteously, and godly in the present age" (Titus 2:12). When we are saved, God's Holy Spirit takes up residence in our lives to guide us into all truth. He works through the Word of God to help us live as people under the authority of our King. We are to walk in newness of life, love, light, and wisdom, obeying our King. If our lives do not increasingly reflect these virtues, we cannot claim to be part of the kingdom of Christ (cf. 1 Corinthians 6:9-10). It does not mean that we cannot be saved, but it does mean that we need to be saved.

Deceivers, Disobedience, and Disassociation (vv. 6-7)

We are not to be deceived by empty words (v. 6). There are many deceivers in the world *and* within church walls. These deceivers can be false teachers who might say that because God is love He will not punish sin. But their words are empty; they have no substance. It is precisely because of "these things" (the evil actions listed in the previous verses) that the wrath of God will come on sinners. Therefore, Christians should not tolerate the influence of evil deceivers or allow them to teach in their churches. Tolerance of such people and practices may be politically correct in these days, but it is not in line with God's standards. So Paul appeals, "Therefore do not be partakers with them" (v. 7). We are not to share in the evil doing of those who have excluded themselves from the kingdom of God by their impurity.

10

WALKING IN LIGHT AND WISDOM

Ephesians 5:8-21

In the first seven verses of this chapter, Paul has contrasted *true love* in which Christians are to walk, with *false love* in which Christians are not to partake. Beginning in verse 8 he explains why they are not to partake of false love. The reason is that when they were saved they were changed from darkness to light. The twin themes of darkness and light are common in Scripture. Satan's realm is called the "power of darkness" in Colossians 1:13. In Ephesians, darkness points to spiritual and moral evil, particularly immorality (4:18; 5:1-8). Light represents truth and righteousness (1:18). God is Light without a trace of darkness (1 John 1:5). His Son came into the world as the Light in order to give light to every man (John 1:9). Those who believe in Him become the light of the world (Matthew 5:14).

Walking as Children of Light (v. 8)

Before they were saved, the Ephesians were not only in the environment of spiritual darkness, they themselves were once darkness. When they were saved, therefore, they did not come *into* the light, they *became* light (v. 8). Christ is the Light, and because they are in Him they are now light also. The truth here is not that they changed location, but that they themselves were transformed from being darkness to being light (vv. 6, 8). The environment where they were was still dark, but in it they were now light. Because they were now light in a dark place, Paul exhorts them to "walk as children of light." Their lives must now conform to their new identity.

The Fruit of the Light (vv. 9-10)

Verse 9 explains that when we walk as children of light, the effect will be that fruit is produced in our lives. Most commentators follow the oldest manuscripts in verse 9 that read "the fruit of the light," a preferable reading. Strictly speaking, light does not bear fruit, but Paul describes Christ's light as producing three graces, or qualities of character: goodness, righteousness, and truth. *Goodness* is moral excellence (see 1 Thessalonians 5:15). God is often described as being "good," especially against a backdrop of evil. Goodness is also described as the fruit of the Spirit (Galatians 5:22). *Righteousness* refers to our righteous acts. The members of our bodies (mind, hands, feet, etc.) are to be instruments of righteousness (Romans 6:13). We are to pursue righteousness and practice it (1 Timothy 6:11; 1 John 2:29). *Truth* is being genuine and honest both in what we say and what we do. These graces in the life of a believer will shine in a world of darkness.

The three qualities of goodness, righteousness, and truth are opposed to the "unfruitful works of darkness," which are evil, unrighteousness, and falsehood. When the "children of light" bear the fruit of the light, they demonstrate that they are the children of God who is light. They also prove what is acceptable, or well-pleasing, to the Lord (v. 10). The word "prove" comes from a word used to test metals for their purity. It is also used in 1 Timothy 3:10 of deacons who must be tested, or proved, before they are publicly recognized. True children of light will constantly be finding out what pleases God as they expose themselves to the light and let it shine into every area of their lives. They will ask, "Does this please the Lord?" because they have to some degree learned Christ and been taught by Him (cf. 4:20; John 3:21).

The Unfruitful Works of Darkness (vv. 11-12)

Believers today, as in New Testament times, live in a world filled with the unfruitful works of darkness. If we walk in the light and the fruit of the light is being produced in our lives, we will easily identify unfruitful works of darkness and avoid participating in them. The unfruitful works of darkness are incompatible with the fruit of the light because they are produced in the kingdom of darkness (Galatians 5:19-25). We are to have "no fellowship" and no part in them. We should note that it is the "works" that we are to avoid, not the people who do them. We should not isolate ourselves from the people of the world. Christians are under constant scrutiny by the world, which is quick to criticize them for the slightest inconsistency.

Instead of participating in the unfruitful works of darkness we are to expose them to the light. The instruction here is specifically aimed at exposing the *works* themselves rather than the *people* who do them. The word *expose* as used in the New Testament means "to bring to light" when it refers to impersonal things. The film in a camera reveals the image when it is exposed to the light. In the same way, the "image" of evil is revealed when it is exposed to the light of Christ (John 3:20). The light of Christ often shines more powerfully through the godly lives, attitudes, and actions of believers than through their words. These are the means by which we let the light in us openly expose sin. We do it this way because the works of darkness are so abhorrent that it is often shameful even to mention them (v. 12). To speak of them would be to assign them some dignity, as if favoring them with attention. Many of these are hidden, immoral, and perverted things that are done in secret (cf. v. 3).

Darkness Becomes Light (vv. 13-14)

Although the exact meaning here is a little obscure, the flow of thought seems to begin with the exposure of the deeds of darkness (v. 11). First, the light reveals the evil deeds. When the deeds are exposed to the light, they become visible. Finally the light transforms them and they become light (v. 13). This process is not a given; sinners are not automatically saved by being exposed to the lives and testimony of believers. The transformation to light depends on response, which was the case in the experience of these Ephesians. Their former sins had been exposed when Paul first visited the city and began preaching the gospel. The light of Christ shined on their sin and led to their salvation. The light not only exposes evil but transforms those who respond to it so that they become light themselves. This view is confirmed by verse 8 where those who were "once darkness" have become "light in the Lord."

Paul concludes his argument on walking in the light with a quotation (v. 14). It uses the same language and imagery as the Old Testament, but it is not a direct quote from Scripture. The quote may possibly allude to "awake" passages in Isaiah (cf. 26:19; 52:1; 60:1) or to the words in Jonah 1:6. Some suggest that these three lines are from an ancient hymn sung by the early church, perhaps in connection with baptism or Easter. The quote seems to refer to our pre-conversion "sleep" in the darkness of spiritual death, our awakening from death to life at conversion, our resurrection to newness of life, and our enlightenment with the light of Christ enabling us to walk in the light.

Walking in Wisdom (vv. 15–21)

In this section, Paul sums up his teaching on walking in a manner worthy of our calling with an admonition to "walk circumspectly," which means to behave wisely, or carefully (v. 15). Unlike the unsaved, whose thinking is futile and whose understanding is darkened (4:17-18), believers have the capacity, through the power of the indwelling Spirit of God, to tread carefully through the spiritual minefield of this world. To choose not to do so is foolish. The contrast between wisdom and foolishness is just as sharp as that between light and darkness covered in the previous section.

Foolishness marks unsaved people. They deny God by their beliefs and practices. Their foolish hearts have been darkened and they have become fools (Romans 1:21-22). In contrast, wisdom begins with the fear of the Lord when we recognize, believe, and obey God (Proverbs 1:7). Wisdom grows as we make choices in the light of the commands in God's Word and as we live like saints who are called to be holy (1:4). David acted "foolishly" when he committed moral sin in disobedience to God's known standards (2 Samuel 24:10). Even the Emmaus disciples were called foolish; they had not "put two and two together" as to what the Old Testament Scriptures had prophesied about Christ (Luke 24:25-26), which accounted for how discouraged and distressed they were. We too act foolishly when we ignore or deliberately fail to obey what God has revealed in His Word. In contrast, we act circumspectly when we believe and obey Him.

"Redeeming the time" (v. 16)

Paul now mentions three things that characterize wise people. The first is that wise people redeem, or make of the best use of, the time and opportunities available to them. God has set boundaries to our lives that limit the opportunities we have to live godly lives and to serve Him. We should make good use of the time available to us because, once time and opportunities are gone, they can never be recovered. In addition, we should redeem the time because the "days are evil." Paul calls these days "this present evil age" (Galatians 1:4). It is an age that is morally wicked and dominated by demonic rulers (1 Corinthians 2:6; Ephesians 2:2). Satan is opposed to God's purpose and seeks to keep us from wisely using the opportunities we have. Wise Christians therefore need to carefully make the best use of their time because the opportunities are limited and the days are evil.

"Understand what the will of the Lord is" (v. 17)

A second thing that marks wise people (in contrast to the foolish) is that they understand what the will of the Lord is. Jesus taught His disciples to pray that God's will be done on earth (Matthew 6:10). Most of God's will for believers in regard to daily living is clearly revealed in His Word. The small percentage of God's will related to special guidance about particular issues in a person's life is usually revealed within the context of obeying the much larger aspects of His will that are contained in the Word. Obedient Christians will sense God's guidance through submission to Him, by prayer, and under counsel from mature believers. This is what it means to be wise in understanding what the will of God is.

"Be filled with the Spirit" (v. 18)

The third mark of believers who act wisely is that they are "filled with the Spirit." Once again Paul compares the foolishness of the old life with the wisdom of the new life in Christ. Pagan life included drunkenness, being under the control of alcohol. It often led to sexual excess in the pursuit of pleasure, which is called dissipation, or debauchery. This brought disorder and misery to the community. In contrast, the new life was to be characterized by being filled with, or controlled by, God's Holy Spirit. Control by the indwelling Spirit leads to a Christ-like character that loves as He loves and serves as He serves. It brings order and peace to the community. In both cases (whether alcohol or Holy Spirit), the influence is external in its results. One has negative and destructive results; the other, positive and constructive results.

When we were saved, the Holy Spirit took up residence within us (1 Corinthians 2:12; 6:19). At the same time He also sealed us as belonging to God and baptized us into the body of Christ (Ephesians 1:13; 4:30; 1 Corinthians 12:13). We took no active role in these events; we were passive participants. But being filled with the Spirit, although the verb form is passive (*be* filled) is a matter of consciously yielding ourselves to His control.

There is a parallel passage to this one in Colossians 3:16 in which the result of letting "the word of Christ" dwell in us richly is that we teach and admonish one another in psalms, hymns, and spiritual songs. In Ephesians 5 the result of being filled with the Spirit is just the same. We could reason, therefore, that being filled with the Spirit is the same as asking the Holy Spirit to take the things of Christ that we read in the Scriptures and to apply them to our lives (John 16:14).

Note that, in contrast to some false teaching today, the work of the Holy Spirit is not orchestrated by special techniques or "step" programs. Also, it is meant to be a continuous process in the experience of all believers and not a "second blessing" reserved for those who pray earnestly for it. Literally, the phrase reads, "be being filled."

The Results of Being Filled by the Holy Spirit (vv. 19-21)

1. Fellowship (v. 19)

There are four beneficial results to those who are filled with Christ and controlled by the Spirit. The first result is that believers who gather together in the fellowship of the local church will speak to one another in psalms and hymns and spiritual songs. They teach and admonish each other inspired by the Spirit who is controlling and directing them. In doing so they are to use "psalms," probably referring to the book of Psalms. They also use "hymns" that exalt biblical truth and "spiritual songs" of testimony and praise. There is no sharp distinction among these, but they describe a full range of spoken and musical praise used in the fellowships of believers to build up, to encourage, and to exhort each other (cf. Colossians 3:16). We can all have a part in doing this by singing out heartily in our song services. In that way we will encourage one another spiritually by our corporate singing.

2. Worship (v. 19)

The second result of being filled with the Spirit is worshipping by "singing and making melody in their hearts to the Lord" (v. 19). It is worship this time because believers sing *to the Lord* and not to each other, as in the first clause. Making music in our heart does not mean worshipping inwardly and silently but with our whole being rather than simply singing with others. Our intellects, wills, and emotions should all be involved. Zacharias was one who was filled with the Spirit and responded by "making melody" saying,

"Blessed is the Lord God of Israel" (Luke 1:67-79). Our churches should be places where we are truly controlled by the Spirit, centering our worship on Christ and involving our whole beings in worship.

3. Thankfulness (v. 20)

The third result of being filled with the Spirit is thankfulness to God the Father at all times and in all circumstances (v. 20). In his own experience, Paul knew what it was to be joyfully thankful, "singing hymns to God" even when chained up in prison (Acts 16:25). Note that Spirit-filled believers are thankful. They express their thanks "to God the Father." It is He who did not spare His only Son but gave Him up for us all. Knowing this, we can be assured that everything He allows in our lives is for our good. Therefore we ought to be thankful. We are to give thanks "always," that is, constantly. We are to give thanks "for all things" because all things work together for good. We are to give thanks "in the name of our Lord Jesus Christ," that is, with His authority, based on who He is and all that He has done for us.

4. Submission to One Another (v. 21)

The fourth result, and one of the great proofs of being filled by the Spirit, is submission to our fellow believers. Submission means that we take the attitude of a servant in putting the needs of others before our own. It is mutual submission by all to all. Those with the more public ministry gifts should be just as ready to receive spiritual encouragement from others as those with the less public gifts. When we are controlled by the Spirit of God and desire to be like Christ, who came not to be served, but to serve, we will count it an honor to submit to one another in the fear of God. The marginal reading, "fear of Christ," is better. This is not just rhetoric; it refers to our proper sense of awe in the presence of Him who is Lord of all and before whom we must appear at the judgment seat (2 Corinthians 5:10).

When we walk in the light we will bear the fruit of the light in all moral goodness, practical righteousness, and truth. When we walk in wisdom, we will understand what the will of the Lord is. When we are filled and controlled by the Spirit, the results will flow in two directions: toward God in worship and thanksgiving, and toward others in warm, interactive fellowship and humble service.

CHAPTER

11

WALKING IN SUBMISSION

Ephesians 5:22-6:9

Paul has been urging the believers in the church to yield to the control of the Holy Spirit. The result will be fellowship, worship, thanksgiving, and mutual submission (vv. 18-21). Paul now takes the fourth of these evidences of the filling of the Spirit and shows how it applies to some basic relationships of life. Function and harmony in relationships require that we submit to those in authority over us while they submit to the higher authority of Christ. Relationships in marriage, home, and workplace are transformed when believers are controlled by the Spirit and show reverence for Christ. Verse 21 is the transition between this control and its result in transformed relationships.

Revolutionary Teaching

When believers in the early church put these Christian principles into practice, they transformed their social conditions for the better, compared to the common practices of the Greco / Roman world. In that day and culture, husbands, parents, and masters were typically domineering and wives, children, and workers were servile. Christian teaching was revolutionary. In marriage it resulted in partnership, holiness, love, and dignity. In parent / child relations it brought warmth, protection, order, and stability. In servant / master relations it brought better work conditions and pay, as well as loyalty.

The transformations were to be based on the roles of *authority* and *submission*. Today these words are loaded with negative connotations because we tend to think of them both as open to abuse. But when authority and submission are regulated with proper limits, as indicated by God in His Word, they become the twin foundations of any ordered society. Both authority and submission are necessary for smoothly functioning relationships.

The roles Paul describes have nothing to do with equality before God or with the dignity of personhood. All believers are equal in dignity and value, but they perform different roles within ordered relationships. It is God who designed leadership for some and submission for others to provide for healthy order within society. Paul focuses on three key relationships: husband / wife; parent / child; and master / servant. In each of these relationships, the key to social order is the higher human / divine relationship in which believers carry out their role as if they were doing it directly for Jesus Christ their Lord. Note the phrases "as to the Lord," "in the Lord," and "as to Christ" (v. 22; 6:1, 5).

The Duties of the Wife in Marriage (vv. 22-23)

Paul begins with the role of the wife. She is to submit to her husband "as to the Lord." This means that in accepting her role of submission to her husband she understands that God gave him his authority. In submitting to him she is really submitting to Christ.

- ✓ The *motive* for her submission to her husband is to honor Christ.
- ✓ The *reason* for her submission is the husband's role as the head of the wife.
- ✓ The *model* for her submission to the headship of her husband is the church's submission to Christ, its head (v. 22, cf. 1:22).

As a wife responds to her husband's godly leadership she acts out the role of the church in relation to Christ. Christ's headship has already been described as assisting the church to grow to full maturity (4:15-16). It is not a controlling tyranny, but a loving, caring leadership. When the church willingly submits to Christ's leadership it can reach the full potential that God designed for it. In the same way, when a godly wife submits to the loving leadership of her husband, she will not only be fulfilled but will accomplish all that God intended for her.

"The Savior of the body" (v. 23)

Still speaking of Christ, Paul goes on to say that "He is the Savior of the body" (v. 23). Some commentators suggest that the term "Savior" may mean protector or provider. In this sense it gives a model for husbands as protectors and providers for their wives. However, the context does not refer to the wife as her husband's body. In addition, the word "Savior" is used exclusively of Christ and God in the New Testament. It is better to see the flow of thought referring to Christ the head of the church, which is His body. As well as being its head He is also the Savior of the church. He gave Himself to die on the cross for the church and became its Lord and Savior (cf. 5:2, 25).

Paul now uses the church's submission to Christ as the model for the wife's role in submission to her husband (v. 24). Note that the responsibility and initiative to submit rests with the wife. In using this analogy, Paul elevates the role of the wife to the highest possible level. Just as the church should gladly acknowledge Christ's authority over it and aim to please Him in every way, so a wife ought also to joyfully embrace and accept her husband's loving authority. Ideally he should not be unreasonable in his demands, and she should not act selfishly. Wives submitting themselves to their husbands would be in sharp contrast to the culture of Ephesus with its enormous temple of the goddess Artemis and its emphasis on the rights of women.

The Duties of Husbands (vv. 25-28)

It is the wife's duty to *submit*, and it is the husband's duty to *love*. These two duties are placed in perfect balance. The husband is to love his wife as Christ loved the church. His duty to love her extends far beyond his natural affection for her; it is to be self-sacrificing love that constantly seeks her welfare. Notice carefully that it is *not* his duty to see that she submits to him so that he might dominate her. What *is* his duty is to love her unselfishly. That kind of love was revealed at the cross where Christ gave Himself up for His bride, the church. Just as Eve was taken from the side of Adam, so the bride of Christ was created, so to speak, from the blood that flowed from the side of the Savior.

Christ's Purpose of Giving Himself for the Church (vv. 26-27)

What was the purpose of Christ sacrificially giving Himself up to purchase the church? There are really two purposes, and both of them go far beyond the relationship between husband and wife. The first was to sanctify it, that is, to make it holy, set apart for Himself (v. 26). It was unholy, so He sanctified it by the truth of the gospel and cleansed it "with the washing of water by the word" (cf. 1 Corinthians 6:11 and Titus 3:5). Then He claimed the church as His bride. His second purpose awaits a future day when He will present the church to Himself in heaven, "holy and without blemish" (v. 27). The church will then be free from all taint of sin. It will be holy and blameless in moral and spiritual beauty when the Bridegroom presents His bride to Himself. What a glorious day that will be! (Revelation 19:7-10).

Why Husbands Are to Love Their Wives (vv. 28-30)

Paul now links the sublime marriage-scene in heaven to the duties of husbands to love their wives. Christ's love for His bride, who is also His body, becomes the standard by which men are to love their wives. "So husbands ought to love their own wives as their own bodies" (v. 28). It is an extension of the second and great commandment, "You shall love your neighbor as yourself" (Leviticus 19:18). Paul now gives the analogy of the love a man has for his own body as a standard for loving his wife. Husbands and wives are "one flesh," that is, one body. Thus he adds, "He who loves his wife loves himself." It means that for him to love her *is actually* to love himself, for she is "one flesh" with him. This means that Christian men should passionately care for their wives just as they do in feeding, maintaining, bathing, clothing, and protecting themselves (v. 29).

This is what the Lord does for His body, the church. The church is so intimately joined with Christ that it is actually part of Him (v. 30). The church should understand how much He loves His body, and husbands should be careful to care as deeply for their wives as they do their bodies (v. 30).

Marriage: an Institution and a Mystery (vv. 31-33)

The subject of being part of His body draws Paul to quote from Genesis 2:24, perhaps the most basic statement in Scripture on the institution of marriage (v. 31). It says that the marriage bond takes precedence over all other human relations and that it is a genuine union between husband and wife: "The two shall become one flesh." Marriage is a beautiful illustration of the church's union with Christ. The standard for marriage, therefore, is that it is sacred and indissoluble.

The relationship of Christ to the church is a "great mystery," a previously unknown truth, but now revealed. The truth concerning Christ and the church was not understood until God revealed it through Paul. The revealed mystery is *the union of Christ and the church* as reflected in the marriage of a Christian man and woman. It emphasizes the relationship between Christ and the church as the standard for the Christian husband and wife.

The whole section is summarized in the last verse of the chapter. Every husband, literally, *each, one by one,* is to love his wife as he loves himself, recognizing that he is one with her. He should ensure that he is worthy of her respect. For her part, the wife is to see that she respects her husband in reverence to the Lord (v. 33).

Children and Parents (6:1-4)

Paul continues his discussion of submission in the relationships of the Spirit-controlled life to give instructions about the relationship of children and parents in the family. He speaks first directly to "children." Commentators rightly point out that Paul must have expected children to be gathered with their families in the church setting where this letter would be read.

Children are commanded to "obey" their parents, a stronger word than the word "submit" applied to wives. Their obedience is to be "in the Lord" or, as the parallel passage has it, "for this is well-pleasing to the Lord" (Colossians 3:20). The reason for their obedience is that it is "right." It is the proper response of children to their parents. When children fail to learn to obey authority at home they will struggle to submit to other authority structures later in life: at school, at work, in relation to police and government, and—most of all—to God. The cumulative effect of disobedience in the home is chaos in society.

Submission to Parental Authority

It therefore becomes the important duty of children to learn to obey their parents. All children are born rebels and their encounter with authority will occur very shortly after birth when they resist the will of their parents. If the clash of wills between parent and child is not resolved, it leads in one of two directions. On the one hand, parents may resort to abusive means to try to force their wills on the child. On the other hand, parents may too quickly capitulate to the child and find that the child's will has been forced on *them*. In both cases, the long-term result is social disaster.

The instruction to children is given by quoting the fifth of the Ten Commandments, "Honor your father and mother" (v. 2; Exodus 20:12). To honor parents includes obedience, but it is more. It means to esteem them highly and to respect them deeply (cf. Exodus 21:15, 17). The fifth commandment is described here as "the first commandment with promise," that is, with a promise attached. This phrase has some interpretive problems, but it is enough here to say that the word "first" should be taken as first in importance for the children to whom it is addressed.

The promise for keeping the commandment was that they would have a long life. This is best understood as a principle for society at large rather than in an individual sense. As a general rule, submission to parents leads to submission to other authority structures, which in turn leads to stability and security in society, which in turn allows life to flourish. This is the concept behind the original giving of the fifth commandment to Israel when they were on the verge of becoming established as a nation and a working society.

The Responsibility of Fathers (6:4)

Fathers, as the heads of families, have a large responsibility in bringing up children. They are instructed here not to provoke their children to anger, which gives rise to resentment and discouragement. This would come about by making unreasonable demands on them in view of their immaturity. It is all too easy for insensitive fathers to use abusive language, to play favorites, to humiliate and ridicule. Many young people have grown up angry at the world because they have taken the brunt of their fathers' anger. Wise fathers will discipline their children with wisdom and balance. They will encourage them to reach their potential with understanding and love, realizing that they are a "heritage from the Lord" (Psalm 127:3).

Fathers are to "bring them up in the training and admonition of the Lord" (v. 4). To *bring up* means to nourish and feed (5:29). It indicates tender affection and loving care. The word *training* is the word for disciplined instruction. It includes "training in righteousness," which is based on Holy Scripture (2 Timothy 3:16). The word *admonish* means verbal correction or confrontation for the purpose of improvement. It is the same word that Paul used in regard to his training of the Ephesians: "I did not cease to warn [admonish] everyone night and day with tears" (Acts 20:31). This is the particular task of fathers with their children.

Servants and Masters (6:5-9)

The conclusion of Paul's application of the Spirit-filled life to household relationships has to do with servants and masters. The "servants" were the lower class of the Roman world. Most of these were employed in households. One third of the population of the Roman Empire were slaves, with a growing number becoming believers. A few, no doubt, were part of Christian households, like Onesimus in the Book of Philemon, but the great majority worked for unbelieving masters. Obviously, many had become an integral part of the church at Ephesus. Paul does not comment on the social custom of slavery; rather, he focuses on the tension they faced between their freedom in Christ and their place in the social system. Paul gave clear instructions concerning God's expectations for them to work as slaves under the control of the Spirit. Even when they could not change their plight, they could walk worthy of the Lord.

As he did with the wife / husband relationship and the child / parent relationship, Paul begins here with the subordinate group, the servants. Once again, submission is the keynote. Their first task was to obey their masters, whether good or bad. They were masters "according to the flesh," that is, they were their earthly masters. Their obedience was to be with "fear and trembling," or in the fear of God, trying not to make any mistake that would bring dishonor on God. Note that the same words are used for all believers in Philippians 2:12. Thus they were to do their very best "as to Christ," or, for His sake.

Serving Two Masters (6:6-8)

Paul invented two compound words, "eyeservice" and "men-pleasers," to describe slaves who only worked hard when their master was watching. This was a great temptation for slaves who were not paid and had no incentive to work. They were to remember instead that they were really "bondservants of Christ" (v. 6) and "doing service, as to the Lord" (v. 7). Behind their earthly master stood their heavenly Master. The slaves in Ephesus were to serve well because by doing so they could do the "will of God from the heart" (v. 6). They could serve with genuine good will, that is, with an attitude of eagerness to please both their earthly and heavenly masters. These teachings are instructive today, for every Christian employee is in a servant / master relationship and should earnestly strive to please his employer and his Lord in his work.

The paragraph closes with a promise that faithful servants who have truly served the Lord in their work will be rewarded in heaven (v. 8). It is to this end that both slaves and free people should serve. Rewards will come at the judgment seat of Christ, where there will be no respect of persons regarding status on earth and where everyone will receive according to what he has done (2 Corinthians 5:10). The kind of service that will be rewarded will be service done with the proper attitude and with the focus on Christ.

Instructions for Masters (6:9)

Paul then addresses the Christian slave owners with instructions that could be applied to employers of every type. He gives three guidelines for dealing with their slaves (or employees). First, they were to "do the same things to them." This means that masters must treat their slaves with "sincerity of heart" (v. 5), "doing the will of God from the heart" (v. 6), and "with good will" (v. 7), "knowing that whatever good anyone does, he will receive the same from the Lord" (v. 8). Second, they were to stop the common practice of misusing their authority with threats of severe punishment and cruelty. Third, they were to recognize that both masters and servants will stand equally accountable before Christ, the impartial judge.

CHAPTER

12

SPIRITUAL WARFARE

Ephesians 6:10-24

Paul has been describing the Christian's walk which, when lived out, glorifies God. Committed Christians can, however, expect spiritual opposition to living such a life because Satan and his hosts are against anything that glorifies God. Aware of this, Paul now moves to describing the Christian's warfare and the armor that God has provided to help the Christian live effectively and victoriously. Paul would easily be reminded of military images because he himself was chained to a soldier while writing to the Ephesians (v. 20). Thus, he illustrates the spiritual warfare of the Christian with terms that both he and his Ephesian readers would be familiar with.

This passage contains the third mention of Satan in the book (2:2; 4:27). With his hosts of fallen angels he is actively engaged today in opposing both God's purpose and His people. He has no power to remove a believer from being "in Christ" but he does have power to stunt his spiritual growth and neutralize his testimony for Christ. In fact, Satan opposes every form of evangelizing the unsaved, every aspect of the individual believer's growth in Christ, and every effort to strengthen the church as a whole.

The Ephesians knew something of satanic presence in their own city. When Paul first went there he was driven out of the synagogue by opposing Jews (Acts 19:8-9). Some mimicked the way in which he cast out evil spirits (Acts 19:13). He was nearly lynched by the pagan business community because the sales of idols began to decline when so many people were saved (vv. 23-41). But Paul did not run. His attitude was that, despite many adversaries, there remained a wide open door for his ministry there (1 Corinthians 16:8-9).

Although the nature of our own spiritual opposition will probably not be like Paul's, the principle holds true that all Christians are in a spiritual battle to a greater or lesser degree. Jesus' earthly ministry began with spiritual warfare when Satan tempted him in the wilderness (Luke 4:2). It also ended with spiritual warfare in the Garden of Gethsemane when He sweat great drops of blood (Luke 22:44). Spiritual warfare will be part of every growing believer's life and ministry.

"Be strong in the Lord" (v. 10)

In preparation for the conflict, we are commanded to "be strong in the Lord," literally, "strengthen yourselves in the Lord." Our ability to conquer sin and obey God in a hostile environment is not in ourselves, but in the Lord. The phrase "in Christ" ("in the Lord" or "in Him") is the key to the believer's new life. Our salvation is in Him; our hope is in Him; our life is in Him; our unity is in Him; our strength is in Him. His strength becomes ours. In chapter 3, Paul prayed that the Ephesian believers would be "strengthened with might through His Spirit in the inner man" (v. 16). God promises us His strength to live for Him amid opposition, but we must recognize our need and avail ourselves of it.

In some older manuscripts the word "finally" is "henceforth" or "for the remaining time," "from here on." Spiritual warfare was going on at the time Paul was writing and will continue until the end. There will be no truce or let-up in the battle until Satan and his hosts are cast into the pit. Until that time we are to be strong "in the Lord." We are to obey by relying on Christ's strength.

"Put on the whole armor of God" (v. 11)

The general exhortation to be strong is followed by a more specific one: to put on the full armor of God. Here, too, there is God's part (because He provides the armor) and our part (because it is up to us to put the armor on). Both God's enabling power and our active participation are necessary for victory. The "whole" armor refers to the complete equipment needed to protect the believer in spiritual battle. It enables us to "stand." Every piece is essential and every piece is spiritual rather than material because the battle is spiritual in nature (2 Corinthians 10:4).

The Demonic Forces of Evil (vv. 11b-12)

Paul identifies our evil and unseen enemies in several categories of fallen angels or demons. The categories seem to refer to the different levels of authority and activity in a hierarchy under Satan. His plan is to destroy the work of God, neutralize the effectiveness of the people of God, and thwart the purpose of God. Each category of evil powers is described in an attack mode against believers. Believers, therefore, are to take a stance against them defensively. Note the word "against" used before each of them.

Satan's name means "slanderer." His "wiles" (scheming) refer to the deceitful means he uses to accomplish his goals (v. 11). As a created being, he can only be in one place at one time, but he does, without doubt, mastermind the attacks carried out by his demonic hosts. He orchestrates their evil work to deceive and seduce using every means at his disposal. In the Gospels he is depicted taking away the Word from people's hearts and using signs and wonders to mislead (Luke 8:12; Matthew 24:24). Here in Ephesians he is shown looking for opportunities to stir up a Christian's anger (4:26-27). His wiles also include moral temptation, doctrinal error, promoting self, discouragement, and confusion. He attacks where we are each most vulnerable. Knowing this should prompt us to be alert to his scheming and to daily put on the armor of God described here.

Principalities and Powers (v. 12)

The principalities and powers refer to high ranks of demons, though their specific functions are not stated (1:21; 3:10; cf. Colossians 2:15; 1 Peter 3:22). The "rulers of the darkness of this age," also translated "world forces of this darkness," are perhaps demons involved with the governmental power structures of the world. Believers have been delivered from the power of darkness (Acts 26:17-18; Colossians 1:13). The final category is called, "spiritual hosts of wickedness in the heavenly places." These may be demons that are involved in gross moral and spiritual evil, such as perverted sexual and occult practices.

What is important is not the identification of the categories but the realization of how evil and powerful these satanic forces are. Note that all three times these authorities are mentioned in Ephesians they are in the "heavenly places" (1:20-21; 3:10; 6:12). They operate in the spiritual sphere.

Heavenly places seem to include a succession of levels, God occupying the highest level and the demonic forces occupying the lowest, sometimes called "the air" (Ephesians 2:2).

"The whole armor of God" (v. 13)

For the second time Paul commands us to "take up the whole armor of God." We do this to enable us to withstand or resist "in the evil day," which is probably similar to the "evil days" of Ephesians 5:16. It refers especially to critical occasions in this present age when evil forces are dominant. When we have "done all," that is, when we have consciously *taken up* and *put on* God's armor, we will be able to resist the attack and stand firm. It is critical that we lose no ground. Our victory is in resisting our enemy and standing firm. Everything we need for victory is found in the armor that God provides. There is no need for any believer to live a defeated life.

"The belt of truth" (v. 14)

The first item of armor we are to take up and put on is the belt of truth. The Roman soldier wore a heavy leather belt around his waist and under his loose outer garment, or tunic. Whenever he marched or fought, he tucked the tunic under the belt securely so that he would be free and unimpeded, ready for any sudden attack.

For the Christian soldier, it is the belt of truth that keeps him prepared for action. As soldiers of Jesus Christ, we need to have a good understanding of the truth of Scripture to counter the lies of the devil. But not only do we need to intellectually *learn the truth* of right doctrine; we also need to experientially *practice the truth*. The practice of truth is a key factor in living victoriously over sin and in trials. When we know and practice truth we are aware of the deceitful tactics of the enemy and less likely to be taken by surprise. Messiah Himself wears the belt of faithfulness and truth (Isaiah 11:5). To have "girded your waist with truth" is to have prepared yourself with truth for the battle (Exodus 12:11; Luke 12:35; 1 Peter 1:13).

"The breastplate of righteousness" (v. 14)

The second piece of armor is the breastplate of righteousness. The breastplate was a thick piece of armor that covered the soldier's entire torso to protect his vital organs. Righteousness, as used here, is the righteousness of character. It is moral righteousness rather than the righteous standing a believer enjoys before God due to his being "in Christ." Paul spoke to the Corinthians of the "armor of righteousness" as being the righteous acts by which he and Timothy commended themselves to be servants of God (2 Corinthians 6:7). In Ephesians, the two previous references to righteousness are to practicing righteous acts (4:24; 5:9). Isaiah pictures God Himself as putting on His righteousness as a breastplate (Isaiah 59:17). In the Psalms, David expresses the close connection between righteousness and winning the battle (Psalm 7:3-5).

The breastplate of righteousness refers to our speech, our thoughts, and our actions that are pleasing to God. By maintaining a righteous walk, we can withstand the attacks of our enemy.

"Having shod your feet with the preparation of the gospel of peace" (v. 15)

Roman soldiers fought wearing thick-soled sandals studded with nails for good traction in combat. They were attached securely with thongs halfway up the shin. These fighting sandals are called "the preparation of the gospel of peace." The references to "feet" and the "gospel of peace" lead many commentators to see an allusion to Isaiah 52:7, which reads, "How beautiful . . . are the feet of him . . . who proclaims peace." In Romans 10:15, Paul quotes this verse again, also in the context of evangelizing. From this, some commentators conclude that this text speaks of our need to be ready to bring the gospel to the world. The difficulty with this interpretation is that Ephesians 6 is about standing against evil powers, not about evangelizing the lost.

In this context, the "preparation of the gospel of peace" teaches that our being ready, or equipped, to fight is based on the gospel of peace. Paul has already emphasized that the gospel results in peace with God and peace between Jew and Gentile (1:13; 3:6; cf. Romans 5:1). When we walk in the conscious light of being at peace with God and our fellow believers, we will walk with assurance of victory. The "sandals" of peace give us such a "firm grip" that we never "slip" in defeat. With such a sure footing, so to speak, we are able to withstand the enemy's attack without anxiety.

"The shield of faith" (v. 16)

Roman soldiers carried a large body shield made of wood and covered with linen and animal hide. It was designed to stop enemy arrows, particularly those shot in the early stages of a battle. Sometimes the arrows were tipped with pitch and lighted before being shot. An incoming barrage of hundreds of flaming arrows was a fearsome sight. If the soldiers thought that flaming arrows were going to be used by the enemy, they immersed their shields in water to soak the leather. When they did this, the arrows were often extinguished on impact. These fire-tipped arrows picture the "wiles of the devil," here called the "wicked one" (cf. v. 11; Matthew 6:13). Satan works through the world system to tempt us to sin through the lust of the flesh, the lust of the eyes, and the pride of life (1 John 2:16). He works through our own sinful natures to tempt us to fear, to doubt, to rebel, and to disobey. He also works through external circumstances such as persecution, family pressure, and disappointments that tempt us to give up living for Christ.

The fiery darts of the devil are designed to weaken our trust in God. To face them we are to take up the shield of faith. It is important to see that we take the shield "above all" or, better, "in addition to" the other pieces of armor. The shield here pictures the believer's faith in God to grasp His unseen resources when under attack, resources like His strength, His promises, and His provision in times of stress. When we actively exercise faith in God and His resources we are protected against the barrage of "fiery darts" from Satan's hosts. Paul has already referred to faith in Ephesians as the means of acquiring God's strength (1:19; 3:16-17). The apostle Peter teaches us to resist the devil "steadfast in faith," that is, with a firm, resolute, confidence in God (1 Peter 5:9). Faith is our deliberate trust in God for needs as they arise.

"The helmet of salvation" (v. 17)

Roman helmets were made of heavy metal and lined with felt. They protected the head from the double-edged swords used effectively by cavalry. Only a battle-ax could penetrate them. The believer's helmet of salvation protects him by giving him Bible-centered assurance of final victory. Satan often attacks our minds with doubts about God's care for us or His capacity to deliver us. Believers who *know* that their salvation is eternally secure in Christ have put their helmets on. They understand that if God is for them, no one can prevail against them (Romans 8:31). Paul used the same imagery when writing to the Thessalonians, encouraging them to put on "as a helmet the hope of salvation" (1 Thessalonians 5:8). They are assured that the program started by God in eternity past will be completed with the triumph of God's Son.

When we have the assurance of certain and complete salvation, we are protected from the enemy's two-edged sword of discouragement and doubt that has disabled so many of God's people.

"The sword of the Spirit" (v. 17)

The soldier's final piece of armor was his sword. This was a short weapon carried by all foot soldiers and it was used for hand-to-hand combat. The Christian soldier's sword is called the "sword of the Spirit, which is the Word of God." The Greek word for "word" in this verse is a spoken—not written—word. When we are tempted to sin, we should call to mind relevant Scriptures and speak them out loud to defend ourselves. This requires that we know and store away God's Word in our minds so we can draw on them when needed. The Word of God becomes a sword in the hand of the Christian soldier to drive back the attacking enemy. The classic illustration is how Jesus used the Word when He resisted the temptation of Satan in the wilderness (Luke 4:1-13). Three times He responded to the subtle and sinful suggestions of Satan by declaring, "It is written . . ." After that, the devil departed (v. 13).

The Full Armor

Our spiritual armor does not consist of some formula for rebuking the spirits in the name of Jesus. It does not involve pronouncing victory over Satan or commanding the evil spirits to leave us. It does not require us to quote certain Scriptures like a mantra. Rather, notice in summary form what the pieces of armor represent for the Christian. The belt speaks of *a sound grasp and practice of truth*. The breastplate speaks of *righteous words and acts*. The shoes speak of *peace and reconciliation* that the gospel brings to believers. The shield speaks of our resolute *trust and confidence in God*. The helmet speaks of *full assurance of salvation*. Finally, the sword speaks of the power of the *skilled use of the Word of God*. These six pieces of spiritual armor are not mysterious or exotic but basic principles of Christian living that will enable us to withstand in this, the evil day.

Praying Always, and Watching (v. 18)

Paul continues his exhortations to stand firm while engaged in spiritual warfare by commanding us to pray. Prayer is not presented as another piece of the Christian's armor. It is more than that. It is the atmosphere in which truth, righteousness, and peace can flourish. It is the means by which we can exercise faith, gain assurance, and apply the Word. Praying in faith pervades the use of all six of the pieces of armor. Praying in faith is thus at the center of the teaching on spiritual warfare and is the closing theme of the letter to the Ephesians. Someone has said that Ephesians begins by lifting us up to the heavenly places and ends by pulling us down to our knees. Prayer is necessary because, having reached the point of grasping the exalted truths revealed in this book, we may be tempted to forget our utter dependence on God. And so Paul reminds us of the need to pray.

There are four universal truths about prayer in this verse, indicated by the word "all."

✓ "All prayer" refers to the many varieties of prayer, such as thanksgiving, confession, petition, intercession, and worship (1 Timothy 2:1). It encompasses the various occasions of prayer (such as public or private) and even different postures of prayer.

✓ "All times" conveys how we should continuously and consciously be dependent on God in every circumstance (Acts 2:42, 2 Timothy 1:3).

✓ "All perseverance" indicates alert watchfulness in prayer (Luke 21:36), the need to be steadfastly praying.

✓ "All saints" indicates that all believers are subjects for prayer. Although, for the most part, we pray for people and needs that are known to us personally, we have the privilege (and even the responsibility) to pray for believers we do not know.

Praying in the Spirit (v. 18)

We should notice particularly that when we pray it is to be "in the Spirit," which means to pray depending on the Spirit. God the Holy Spirit helps us to pray even when we can do little but to sigh, "Oh, God," concerning a situation (Romans 8:26-27). To pray in the Spirit is prayer in the context of a spiritual battle (cf. Jude 20). It is to pray under the influence of the Spirit, that is, with the Spirit's direction as well as with our own minds (1 Corinthians 14:15). Praying in the Spirit is sometimes linked with praying in tongues, but there is no suggestion of that in this text.

Our greatest problems, like those of the Ephesian believers, are spiritual and thus the greatest thrust of our prayer life should be toward spiritual needs. In the context of Ephesians 6, our spiritual victory over spiritual foes is of primary concern. It is vital that we pray about our own (and others) spiritual needs, not just physical situations.

Praying for Utterance and Boldness (vv. 19-20)

Paul asked the Ephesians to pray not only for all the saints but especially for him, that he might be given utterance and courage (v. 19). *Utterance* seems to refer to clear speech. Paul needed both the ability to speak the gospel message clearly and the courage to give it, particularly anticipating his defense before Caesar in Rome. What he hoped to communicate clearly to Caesar was the "mystery" that had stirred up such hostility against him from his own people, the Jews. The mystery, as you will remember, was the good news of the grace of God that Gentile believers were fellow heirs with Jewish believers to form the church, one company of God's people (3:6-9).

Paul describes himself as an "ambassador in chains" (v. 20). As God's ambassador he was in Rome, the seat of power in the world at that time in history. It was his job to represent God and the kingdom of God to the authorities. On the way to Rome as a prisoner, the angel had told Paul that he was to be brought before Caesar. Thus he calls himself "an ambassador in chains" (Acts 27:23-24). His own safety was not even in view. What did the chains matter if he could speak clearly and courageously before Caesar? We get some insight into how God answered when he later told Timothy, "The Lord stood with me and strengthened me in order that through me the proclamation might be fully accomplished" (2 Timothy 4:17, NASB).

Personal Greetings (vv. 21-24)

A Christian brother from the province of Asia named Tychicus was with Paul in Rome while he wrote this letter. He had been a trusted courier of the gift from Gentile churches that Paul had taken to Jerusalem (Acts 20:4). He was the courier of this letter and the one to the Colossians. Later, during his second imprisonment, Paul sent him again to Ephesus and possibly to Crete (2 Timothy 4:12; Titus 3:12). All this confirms Paul's description of Tychicus as a beloved brother and faithful servant. When he arrived in Ephesus he would explain Paul's situation more fully and also comfort and encourage these local believers.

Paul closes with a benediction (v. 23). He desires that the brethren may experience the spiritual blessings of peace, love, and faith, all of which, as he has gone to great lengths to explain, are gifts from the hand of God. Finally, he prays for grace, his usual benediction, on all those who love our Lord Jesus Christ. The term "in sincerity" is ambiguous in the Greek and may be better rendered "incorruptible." It is fitting that Paul closes by conveying the blessing of grace on those believers in Christ whose heartfelt desire is to know and love their Savior in a deeper and fuller way.

NOTES

NOTES

NOTES

NOTES